SICILIAN FEASTS

The Hippocrene Cookbook Library

Afghan Food & Cookery
Alps, Cuisines of the
Aprovecho: A Mexican-American
    Border Cookbook
Argentina Cooks!, *Exp. Ed.*
Austrian Cuisine, Best of, *Exp. Ed.*
Belarusian Cookbook, The
Bolivian Kitchen, My Mother's
Brazil: A Culinary Journey
Burma, Flavors of
Cajun Cuisine, Stir the Pot: The History of
Cajun Women, Cooking with
Calabria, Cucina di
Caucasus Mountains, Cuisines of the
Chile, Tasting
China's Fujian Province, Cooking from
Colombian Cooking, Secrets of
Croatian Cooking, Best of, *Exp. Ed.*
Czech Cooking, Best of, *Exp. Ed.*
Danube, All Along The, *Exp. Ed.*
Egyptian Cooking
English Country Kitchen, The
Estonian Tastes and Traditions
Filipino Food, Fine
Finnish Cooking, Best of
French Fashion, Cooking in the (*Bilingual*)
Germany, Spoonfuls of
Greek Cooking, Regional
Greek Cuisine, The Best of, *Exp. Ed.*
Gypsy Feast
Haiti, Taste of
Havana Cookbook, Old (*Bilingual*)
Hungarian Cookbook, *Exp. Ed.*
Icelandic Food & Cookery
India, Flavorful
Indian Spice Kitchen, The, *Exp. Ed.*
International Dictionary of Gastronomy
Irish-Style, Feasting Galore
Jewish-Iraqi Cuisine, Mama Nazima's
Korean Cuisine, Best of
Laotian Cooking, Simple
Latvia, Taste of
Lebanese Cookbook, The
Ligurian Kitchen, A
Macau, Taste of
Mexican Culinary Treasures
Middle Eastern Kitchen, The

Naples, My Love for
Nepal, Taste of
New Hampshire: from Farm to
    Kitchen
New Jersey Cookbook, Farms and
    Foods of the Garden State:
Norway, Tastes and Tales of
Ohio, Farms and Foods of
Persian Cooking, Art of
Pied Noir Cookbook: French
    Sephardic Cuisine
Piemontese, Cucina: Cooking from
    Italy's Piedmont
Poland's Gourmet Cuisine
Polish Cooking, Best of, *Exp. Ed.*
Polish Country Kitchen Cookbook
Polish Cuisine, Treasury of (*Bilingual*)
Polish Heritage Cookery, *Ill. Ed.*
Polish Holiday Cookery
Polish Traditions, Old
Portuguese Encounters, Cuisines of
Pyrenees, Tastes of
Quebec, Taste of
Rhine, All Along The
Romania, Taste of, *Exp. Ed.*
Russian Cooking, Best of, *Exp. Ed.*
Scottish-Irish Pub and Hearth
    Cookbook
Sephardic Israeli Cuisine
Sicilian Feasts
Slovenia, Flavors of
South Indian Cooking, Healthy
Spanish Family Cookbook, *Rev. Ed.*
Sri Lanka, Exotic Tastes of
Swedish Kitchen, A
Taiwanese Cuisine, Best of
Thai Cuisine, Best of Regional
Trinidad and Tobago, Sweet Hands:
    Island Cooking from
Turkish Cuisine, Taste of
Tuscan Kitchen, Tastes from a
Ukrainian Cuisine, Best of, *Exp. Ed.*
Uzbek Cooking, Art of
Vietnamese Kitchen, A
Wales, Good Food from
Warsaw Cookbook, Old

SICILIAN FEASTS

Giovanna Bellia La Marca

HIPPOCRENE BOOKS
NEW YORK

*This book is dedicated to the Bellia, Biazzo, Sirugo,
La Marca, and Sacco families.*

Acknowledgments:
I would like to thank Howard La Marca for his unconditional faith, Nicoletta La Marca Sacco for inspiring me, Steven Sacco for being my computer guru, Gary A. Goldberg of The New School for showing me the way, and Anne E. McBride, my editor at Hippocrene, for making it happen.

Book and jacket design by Acme Klong Design, Inc.

For more information, address:
Hippocrene Books, Inc.
171 Madison Ave.
New York, NY 10016
www.hippocrenebooks.com

Library of Congress Cataloging-in-Publication Data

La Marca, Giovanna Bellia.
    Sicilian feasts / Giovanna Bellia La Marca.
        p. cm.
    Includes bibliographical references and index.
    ISBN-10: 0-7818-0967-3
    ISBN-13: 978-0-7818-0967-2
    1. Cookery, Italian--Sicilian style. I. Title.

TX723.M293 2003
641.59458--dc21

2003049930

Printed in the United States of America.From Hippocrene's Sicilian Library

TABLE OF CONTENTS

Ragusa – Ponte Vecchio. Ragusa has three bridges: Ponte Nuovo, Ponte Vecchio, and Ponte San Vito. This photograph is taken from Ponte Nuovo and it shows the other two bridges.

To my great delight, my grandmother Concettina Biazzo Bellia allowed me to "help" her in the kitchen even as a very young child. That was before my family emigrated to the United States from Ragusa, Sicily, when I was 10 years old.

Ragusa is the southernmost city in Sicily, located on a mountain near the point of the triangle, which is the shape of the island, 10 miles from the Mediterranean Sea. Ragusa, together with eight other cities in the nearby area, has been listed by UNESCO, an agency of the United Nations that works to protect cultural and natural treasures in 125 countries, as a World Heritage Site. Ragusa and the other eight towns were destroyed by an earthquake in 1693, so their reconstruction represents important innovations in seventeenth and eighteenth century urban planning. When Ragusa was rebuilt, the plan of the city was created with the "modern" technique of parallel north-south streets going up the mountain that are perpendicular to the streets going east-west. This is a contrast to the streets of the ancient section of the city, Ragusa Ibla, in which, to this day, the streets follow the contour of the land, and no two are parallel to each other. The earthquake spared the portal of the medieval church of San Giorgio, which still stands and is the symbol of the city. The new church, designed in the baroque style, was built on higher ground on top of a majestic staircase.

Ragusa Ibla – Portal of San Giorgio – This portal is all that remained standing of the medieval church of San Giorgio after the earthquake of 1693. This portal is the symbol of the city.

Ragusa Ibla hosts an important international music competition, The Ibla Grand Prize, which takes place annually during the last week of June and the first week of July. Under the direction of founder and director Salvatore Moltisanti, a young, energetic and very talented virtuoso of the piano, hundreds of musicians come to Ragusa Ibla from all over the world and perform to a delighted public as they compete for the awards. The winners perform in New York the spring following the competition.

During my childhood in Ragusa, I learned to appreciate the history, the natural beauty, the mystery of the mountains, the beautiful baroque architecture, and the food of a city that has had continued habitation for over two thousand years.

As an adult, I developed a passion for cooking and serving all sorts of dishes, but particularly the food of my birthplace.

Ragusa – Cathedral of San Giovanni

3

I have collected, tested, and researched recipes during and after my frequent trips to Italy and to Sicily. I have been assisted in this by the generosity of friends and family who have enthusiastically parted with their traditional and treasured family recipes.

In July of 1997, I was asked by the Rotary Club of Ragusa to be part of a three-member jury for a cooking competition between the cities of Ragusa and Modica. The competition was held on a lovely country estate near Modica, and it attracted some of the finest cooks in the southeastern part of Sicily. I felt qualified to be a judge since I was born in Ragusa, and my grandfather Don Giovannino Sirugo, who was an excellent cook, was born in Modica. As my family members tease, I have cooking in my genes!

My father, Felice Bellia, and his mother Concettina were enthusiastic cooks. My maternal grandfather's own father had been a *monzu'*, a professional cook at the Castle of Donnafugata, now a museum, and later at the Monastery of Il Carmine in Ragusa. *Monzu'*, which is a corruption of the French *monsieur*, was the title earned by a class of professional cooks who developed a very refined and rather elaborate cuisine, and who were employed either by aristocratic families, or by the church. A wealth of recipes and cooking techniques has been handed down to me, which I've always enjoyed using and would like to share.

Now that more people are traveling to Sicily, I would like to inspire Americans to try some of our delicious traditional recipes, especially the foods they enjoyed while visiting there. Since we are able to get just about any ingredient in the United States, either at local Italian groceries, through mail order, or on the Web, the home cook can be adventurous in trying interesting and even exotic recipes. Most home cooks have labor-saving appliances that the *monzu'* of the eighteenth and nineteenth centuries would have welcomed and used in his kitchen had they been available. It is the availability of ingredients and equipment that makes it possible for the home cook to reproduce even the most elaborate historical dishes.

Cooking has always been central to my life, both for my family, and for my family of friends. Since my professional training is in design, I have always enjoyed presenting even the most humble fare creatively. Sharing cooking techniques and recipes, making suggestions for entertaining, and creating menus for special occasions has led me to compile a cookbook that combines traditional dishes, foods associated with particular feast days, and some of the elaborate dishes from the kitchens of the *monzu'* that will wow the most exacting guest. But most of all, it's my wish to introduce the American cook to the delights of the varied, ancient, and delicious cuisine of Sicily.

THE FOOD OF SICILY

With increasingly greater numbers of people visiting Sicily to enjoy the history of the island, the ancient Greek temples, the landscape with its hill towns, the natural beauty of the mountains, the sandy beaches, and the beautiful cities, visitors rave about the delicious food of this region of Italy. At a time of great interest in healthful, nutritious, and appealingly interesting foods, the cooking of Sicily provides a wealth of tasty and wholesome recipes. Sicily is the largest island in the Mediterranean Sea, and its cuisine is among the oldest in Europe, a fact that is amply documented in the history of the island.

Four hundred years before the birth of Christ, Plato was engaged by the Tyrant of Syracuse, Sicily, as the teacher for his son Dionisius the Younger. Plato tutored the young man for three months before returning to Greece. Plato deplored the time and attention that was devoted to the preparation and consumption of food in Sicily, and he was distressed by the Sicilian's love for food. He was convinced that in the midst of such decadence and self-indulgence, the youth would surely come to no good. Plato must not have disliked desserts, because he forgave the Sicilians for their sweet tooth, conceding that sweets were the great contribution of Sicilian gastronomy to the ancient world.

Sicilians knew about "nouvelle cuisine" 2,300 years ago when Archestrato, the James Beard of his time, cautioned against making sauces too rich. He recommended reducing condiments to the foods' own juices, and to adding a savory mixture of fresh aromatic herbs chopped and mixed with good olive oil, salt, and sesame seeds.

The appeal that Sicilian cooking has for us today is that it is a simple, flavorful, unpretentious cuisine dependent on uncompromisingly fresh ingredients in season and at the peak of flavor. The techniques of everyday cooking are simple and are aimed at preserving the flavor, texture, and wholesomeness of the fresh ingredients. The Sicilian cook's ingenuity is his or her greatest asset. Many recipes and variations can be made from the humblest vegetables, elevating them to holiday fare.

There are wonderful recipes that are made to celebrate the various holidays of the year. Easter Sunday/Monday offers a double celebration. The centerpiece of the Easter Sunday menu is the traditional 'mpanata ri agnieddu, a delectable lamb pie that will reward the adventurous cook who is willing to try it. This lamb pie is made with a bread crust that encloses well-seasoned lamb stewing meat, bones and all. The meat juices soak into the bottom crust as the pie slowly cools, making it a very flavorful and tasty morsel.

The Easter feast continues on Monday, when people pack a delicious lunch and head for the country or more commonly, to their vacation home in the countryside or at the nearest beach to celebrate *Pasquetta*.

Sicily, which in ancient Roman times was called the "granary of the Italic peninsula," still produces some of the best durum wheat in Italy. Bread and pasta continue to be important to the daily diet, and are of excellent quality. Rice, although not as important a food as it is in the northern provinces, nevertheless appears in some very special dishes. The most memorable for those who have traveled to Sicily is *Arancini*, a very popular finger food. *Arancini* are rice balls stuffed with cheese or meat, covered with bread crumbs, and deep-fried to a golden orange, hence the name that means "little oranges."

The Sicilian dessert table is a delight for the eye as well as for the palate. Beautiful and delicious desserts are known and appreciated all over the world. They include marzipan fruits; ricotta-filled cannoli; spectacular cakes decorated with candied fruits; cookies filled with dried fruits, nuts, and honey; and perhaps the best known dessert, granita, a smooth and refreshing fruit ice that can be made at home quite easily and with fantastic results.

My grandmothers, Concettina and Milina, always said that Sicilians would eat well if they had eggs, flour, dried legumes, and fresh vegetables. Historically, these simple ingredients were the mainstays of Sicilian cooking. Ingredients need not be expensive, and cooking techniques needn't be complicated in order to eat well. To raise this simple cooking to cuisine, I would add good olive oil to the list, the best cold-pressed extra-virgin olive oil you can afford to buy. I grew up watching my mother, father, and grandmothers making feasts out of the most humble and inexpensive ingredients.

Sicilian dishes have great versatility, and are easy to make. Our sauces utilize flavorful and aromatic cooking juices and we don't use stocks for our soups because we depend on the fresh ingredients, a sprinkle of salt, and a drizzle of excellent extra-virgin olive oil to make all the difference.

ABOUT BREAD DOUGH

Bread dough can be made in a mixer equipped with a dough hook, in a bread machine, in a food processor, or in the old-fashioned way, by hand. Contrary to popular opinion, bread dough improves in flavor if it rises slowly in a cool place. I let it rest overnight in a cool place or in the refrigerator. Bread dough can be refrigerated for up to three days. For a delicious snack, take pieces of dough the size of a walnut, flatten it with your hands, and fry until lightly golden in canola or vegetable oil. Sprinkled with salt it is delicious; sprinkled with sugar it becomes a dessert.

YEAST

I use SAF Gold Instant Yeast for all my baking. This yeast is mixed with the flour rather than with the water, so it's not necessary to proof it before mixing it into the recipe. It's designed to give a good rise with sweet doughs as well as with sourdoughs. I use it as an all-purpose yeast. You can substitute an equal amount of active dry yeast for any of the recipes. If you use dry east, mix it with warm water in the amount called for in the recipe. Either type is available from the King Arthur Baker's Catalogue; please check the Appendix.

EXTRA-VIRGIN OLIVE OIL

Extra-virgin olive oil comes from the first cold pressing of the olives. It's the most flavorful and the most healthful. I tell my friends who want to learn to cook as the Sicilians do not to worry about herbs and spices, but to just buy the best extra-virgin olive oil they can afford, because it's so basic to our flavorful cooking. Although olive oil is generally used in cooking a recipe, there are many dishes such as soups, vegetables, and salads that are finished with a drizzle of uncooked extra-virgin olive oil. It's this last addition of olive oil to a dish that gives it a richness of flavor that no amount of flavorings used during the cooking process can equal. Some restaurants now serve a little dish of extra-virgin olive oil to dip bread in, and customers are beginning to really appreciate and enjoy the taste and the flavor of good, uncooked olive oil as Sicilians have done for centuries.

VEGETABLE OIL

Use canola oil, peanut oil, or soybean oil for deep-frying, or for pan-frying eggplant or fritters. Since they absorb some of the oil, olive oil would be too strong a flavor, and it would be too costly.

LARD

Lard, like butter, is an animal product. In Sicily, lard is used to make pastry tender, flaky, and flavorful. If you hesitate to use it because you think that it's bad for your health, you should know that it's nutritionally equal to butter, and a small amount goes a long way. Vegetable shortening can be substituted in any of the recipes.

BASIL

Use only fresh basil. If it's not available omit from the recipe, but don't use dried basil, it will give the dish an off flavor. Grow it in the garden or in a pot, or buy it in the summer, and freeze it for the winter in the form of pesto. I process the basil leaves, and I add enough extra-virgin olive oil to make a thick paste. I freeze it in 4 to 6 ounce jars; baby food jars are perfect.

OREGANO

Use dried oregano, not fresh (which has very little flavor). This herb tastes better after it's been dried. However, use very sparingly. Some people think that using lots of oregano is synonymous with Italian cooking. Wrong. Use very little and only for certain dishes.

PARSLEY

Use only Italian flat-leaf parsley; American curly parsley and cilantro are not substitutes.

SUGAR

Granulated Sugar: the most common sugar; purchased at any supermarket.
Sparkling White Sugar: this glittery large crystal sugar adds sparkle as well as crunch to cookies and cakes, and will not melt when baked.
Pearl Sugar: white tiny chunks of sugar that will add crunch to baked goods and will not melt in the oven.
Powdered Sugar: very finely ground sugar without additives. You can make it at home by processing regular granulated sugar.
Confectioners' Sugar: powdered sugar that has a little cornstarch added so that it doesn't cake up in the box.
Sprinkles, Nonpareils, or Hundreds and Thousands: tiny sugar spheres in mixed colors used to decorate iced cookies and frosted cakes, and some fried confections.

I like to fill my sugar bowls with colored sugar crystals. Place $1/2$ cup sparkling white sugar in a jar with a tight fitting lid. Add a few drops of liquid food color, mix with a spoon, then cover the jar and shake to distribute the color evenly. This will keep indefinetly. You can do green and red for Christmas, pastel colors for the spring, and mix the colored sugars as you wish. To give away as gifts, I layer the different colors in a tall thin glass jars, fill each jar to the very top, cover with a cork and tie a ribbon around the neck of the bottle.

All of these sugars are available from the King Arthur Baker's catalogue; please check the Appendix.

PASTA COOKING WATER

When straining pasta, always save some of the cooking water until you are finished seasoning the dish. Use the cooking water to dilute sauces and to moisten the pasta.

PRICKLY PEARS

I was surprised when I found out that the ubiquitous prickly pear that is found everywhere in Sicily actually came from the New World. They are called *ficupali* in Sicilian and *fichi d'India* (Indian figs) in Italian, so I had always thought that they were native to the Mediterranean region. Prickly pears are the fruit of a cactus plant, so they need to be handled with care. To peel the fruit, cut the top and the bottom so that the pieces remain attached on both ends. Then make a cut down the remaining strip of skin, and extract the fruit. The color of the fruit ranges from chartreuse to magenta. The pulp is similar in texture to watermelon, but is full of little seeds that cannot be removed. Bite into the fruit, let it melt into your mouth enjoying the sweetness, and swallow its seeds and pulp without chewing it. Next time you see them at the supermarket, don't be afraid to try one.

Gole d'Alcantara – a spectacular gorge

APPETIZERS

Rapi pitittu

Siracusa

Most people agree that the antipasti are often the best part of a meal. They are savory, tasty, and sometimes spicy, and eaten with a good piece of bread. Dipping the bread into the delicious juices, you could make a meal of it.

In general, antipasti keep well in the refrigerator, but for best flavor they should be served at room temperature. Before the days of refrigeration, food was preserved suttu sali, in salt, such as capers; sutt'uogghiu, under olive oil with the food literally submerged under the oil; and sutt'acitu, submerged under vinegar. Vegetables were kept for months under oil or vinegar. When I go to Sicily I buy little plastic disks with legs that are used to keep food under the oil or vinegar about one inch under the screw top of the jar. Most of the appetizer recipes will keep for at least two weeks, and many for over a month in the refrigerator.

Most of these recipes depend on very simple ingredients, and relatively few spices for their flavor. When a recipe calls for parsley, it must be Italian flat-leaf parsley, not the curly variety and certainly not cilantro, which is entirely different. Parsley, basil, and mint are always used fresh; if you don't have them, simply leave them out. Oregano, on the other hand is always used dried, because drying it makes more distinctive and flavorful. But use oregano very sparingly, as nothing ruins a dish more than too much of this herb.

If you have a selection of antipasti in your refrigerator, arranging small quantities in a lazy Susan and serving them with slices of bread makes a wonderful and varied presentation for a dinner, to accompany drinks, or for a party. They are the original fast food.

SEASONED BREAD

Pani cunzatu

Serves 6 to 8

1 loaf Italian bread

4 tablespoons olive oil

Salt and red pepper flakes
   to taste

Pinch of dried oregano

Cut the bread in half lengthwise drizzle with olive oil, and sprinkle with salt, red pepper flakes, and just a touch of oregano.

FRIED CHEESE

Caciu frittu

Serves 4 to 6

Caciocavallo, which is imported from Ragusa, and also known as Ragusano, is now easily available in Italian markets. Hard provolone, not the kind sliced for sandwiches, can be substituted.

1 pound caciocavallo cheese

¼ cup extra-virgin olive oil

Cut the cheese in ¼ inch slices. Heat the oil, preferably in a nonstick frying pan. Add the cheese slices in a single layer, and fry until golden before turning to brown the other side. Serve at once.

OVEN-DRIED TOMATOES
Pumarori salati

Makes one pint

Cut the tomatoes in half lengthwise and place in a jelly-roll pan, cut side up. Sprinkle the tomatoes with salt, and place in a 200-degree oven for 12 to 14 hours or until the tomatoes are dried but still pliable. Cool to room temperature, place in a jar with fresh basil leaves between the layers, if desired, and cover with olive oil.

2 pounds Italian plum tomatoes

Kosher salt as needed

Fresh basil leaves (optional)

1 cup extra-virgin olive oil, or more as needed

After the tomatoes have been consumed, the flavored oil is delicious to dip bread in or to pour over pasta, vegetables, or salad. Because these tomatoes are not completely dried, they are perishable, but will keep in the refrigerator for about three weeks if they are submerged in the olive oil.

ROASTED PEPPERS
Pipi arrustuti

Serves 6 to 8

4 green or red bell peppers

2 cloves garlic, chopped

¼ cup extra-virgin olive oil

Salt to taste

Place each of the bell peppers on one of your four gas burners. If you have an electric stove, use the broiler. Cook and turn the bell peppers until each one is black all over. As each one is done, place it in a paper bag so that it steams, and the charred skin peels away easily. Let the cooked bell peppers cool. Remove and discard the core and the seeds, rub away the thin black skin, tear the bell peppers into strips, and place them in a bowl. Dress them with the chopped garlic, olive oil, and salt to taste. Mix them well, and spoon into a jar with a lid. They will keep in the refrigerator for up to 2 weeks. Serve at room temperature.

FELICE'S FRIED BLACK OLIVES

Ulivi fritti

Serves 6 to 8

My father, Felice Bellia, was a fine cook, and this is one of his recipes. The olives are delicious, and so is a piece of bread dipped in its juices!

4 cloves garlic

¼ cup extra-virgin olive oil

½ pound oil-cured black olives

1 tablespoon fennel seeds

2 tablespoons red wine vinegar

Peel the garlic, slice it thinly lengthwise, and fry in the oil until crisp but not burned. Remove and set aside. Add the olives and the fennel seeds to the same pan, lower the heat, and shake the pan for about 1 minute. Holding a cover over the pan, add the vinegar and quickly set the cover on the pan to prevent splashing. Shake the pan for another 30 seconds, and turn off the heat. Place the olives in a serving platter, and top with the crisp fried garlic. These will keep in the refrigerator for up to 3 weeks. Serve at room temperature.

GREEN OLIVE SALAD

Ulivi cunzati

Serves 6 to 8

My mother Concetta made olives into this delicious salad. She even had a special smooth stone to crack them open; nothing else would do!

1 pound whole green olives with pits

4 stalks celery

4 cloves garlic

½ teaspoon dried oregano

Red pepper flakes to taste

½ cup extra-virgin olive oil

¼ cup red wine vinegar

Hit the olives one at a time with a stone or with meat pounder (*batticarne*) to crack them open. Without removing the pits, place them in a jar that will hold them all together with the sliced celery. Crush the garlic, remove the skin, and add to the jar. Add the oregano, red pepper flakes, olive oil, and vinegar. Cover the jar with a screw top, and turn a few times to mix everything. This olive salad will keep in the refrigerator for up to 3 weeks. Serve at room temperature.

CONCETTA'S EGGPLANT WITH MINT

Mulinciana ca' menta

Serves 6 to 8

2 eggplants

1 cup white vinegar

1 tablespoon salt

4 cloves garlic, chopped

10 sprigs fresh mint, chopped

½ cup extra-virgin olive oil

Cut each eggplant into 8 wedges without peeling it. Cut each wedge into 1-inch pieces, and set aside. Bring 2 cups water, the vinegar, and salt to the boil. Add the eggplant, and cook for 7 to 10 minutes or until tender. Strain, and place on a towel to cool and dry.

Place the eggplant in a jar and add the garlic, mint, and olive oil. Cap the jar with a screw top, and give it a few turns to mix everything. This will keep in the refrigerator up to 3 weeks.

Concetta Sirugo and Felice Bellia, 1938

EGGPLANT RELISH

Capunatina

Serves 8 to 10

Tomato catsup in **capunatina** *is my secret ingredient; it might scandalize a Sicilian cook, but because it contains tomato, sugar, and spices, it's a perfect ingredient for this dish. Plain tomato sauce can be substituted if desired.*

Caponata is a delicious accompaniment to meats and is wonderful in sandwiches since it marries well with meats and cheeses. It's even excellent on hot dogs and hamburgers.

1 eggplant

¾ cup olive oil

2 green or red bell peppers, sliced

2 onions

4 stalks celery

2 tablespoons capers, either salted or in vinegar

¼ cup tomato catsup

¼ cup red wine vinegar

Cube the unpeeled eggplant and fry in ½ cup of the olive oil. Spoon into a bowl. Add 2 tablespoons oil to the pan, and add the bell peppers. Sauté until tender and add to the cooked eggplant.

Slice the onions, cut the celery in ½-inch slices, add the capers, and fry in the remaining 2 tablespoons of olive oil. Return the eggplant and the bell peppers to the frying pan, and add the tomato catsup and vinegar. Cook for 2 minutes, and stir to mix the flavors. Cool before serving. This will keep for up to 2 weeks in the refrigerator. Serve at room temperature.

CAPONATA APPETIZERS

Crustini ca' capunatina

Serves 6 to 8

1 loaf Italian bread, thinly sliced

¼ cup extra-virgin olive oil, or olive oil spray

1 cup capunatina (page 17)

Spray or brush the bread slices on both sides, with olive oil. Place in a pan, and toast in a 350 degree oven until the slices begins to brown. Remove from the oven, top each slice with a teaspoonful of capunatina and arrange on a platter.

STUFFED ARTICHOKES

Carciuofili cini

Serves 4 to 8

4 artichokes

1½ cups dried bread crumbs

¼ cup plus 3 tablespoons of extra-virgin olive oil

½ cup grated pecorino cheese

2 cloves garlic, finely chopped

¼ cup chopped Italian flatleaf parsley

Salt and black pepper to taste

To make the stuffing: Place the bread crumbs in a small frying pan, add 3 tablespoons of olive oil, and mix with a wooden spoon over medium heat until golden. Immediately remove from the frying pan as the bread crumbs burn easily at this point just from the heat of the pan. Pour the toasted bread crumbs into a bowl. Add the cheese, garlic, parsley, salt, and pepper and set aside.

Wash the artichokes. Cut away all but ½ inch of the stems. Cut away the top ½ inch of each artichoke. With a pair of kitchen shears, cut away the tips of the remaining leaves, and gently open up the leaves. Starting with the outside and working towards the center, spoon a little bit of filling in each leaf. Pour 1 cup of water in the bottom of a pot that will hold all 4 artichokes. Stand the stuffed artichokes in the pot, drizzle the remaining ¼ cup olive oil over each one. Cover, and place over medium heat. Cook for 35 to 40 minutes or until a leaf separates easily from one of the artichokes. Serve at room temperature. Each artichoke can be cut in half to serve as an appetizer.

STUFFED MUSHROOMS

Funci cini

Serves 6 to 8

16 mushrooms

½ cup extra-virgin olive oil

Stuffing from Stuffed Artichokes
(page 18)

Preheat the oven to 375 degrees. Wash the mushrooms and separate the caps from the stems. Chop the stems, and brown in 2 table-spoons of olive oil. Add the browned mush-room stems, to the prepared stuffing. Divide the stuffing among the 16 mushrooms, place them in an oiled or sprayed baking pan, and drizzle the remaining olive oil over each one. Bake for 35 to 40 minutes or until golden brown. Serve hot or at room temperature.

CHICKPEA FRITTERS

Panelle

Serves 6

An old Italian proverb admonishes "Mazze e panelle fanno i figli belli, panelle senza mazze, fanno i figli pazzi." Discipline and panelle (treats) make children good, but panelle without discipline makes children wild. When my 3½-year-old grandson Felice was on a gluten free diet, panelle became his favorite "bread;" his sister Francesca, who was not quite one, loved them too!

1 cup chickpea flour

3 cups canola oil

Salt to taste

Mix the chickpea flour and 2 cups cold water making sure that there are no lumps. Place on the stove, and bring to the boil while stirring continually. Lower the heat and cook, stirring, constantly until the mixture thickens and leaves the sides of the pan. Take off the heat, and spread on a greased cookie sheet about ½ inch thick. Let cool, cut into 1½-inch strips and then into diamonds.

Heat the canola oil, and deep-fry the panelle until golden. Place on paper towels to absorb the excess oil, sprinkle with salt, and serve hot.

SICILIAN RICE BALLS

Arancini

Makes about 16

Although arancini can be filled with meat and sauce, my mother Concetta, who made them to perfection, liked to prepare them this way. Coating the arancini with flour paste and bread crumbs, and chilling before frying them, was her way of ensuring that they did not crack or open up when deep-fried.

2 cups Italian arborio or American Carolina rice

1 cup Meat Sauce (page 82)

1 cup grated caciocavallo or Romano cheese

1 (10-ounce) package frozen peas, thawed

2 eggs

1 pound ricotta

1 cup flour

2 cups dried bread crumbs

3 cups canola or vegetable oil for deep-frying

Boil the rice until tender and drain. When the rice is still hot, but cool enough to handle, add the sauce, cheese, peas, and eggs, mix well and let cool. Take a handful of rice, make a depression in the middle, and fill with 1 teaspoon of ricotta. Cover the ricotta with more rice, and shape into a ball. As you shape the arancini, place them on a tray.

When you have finished making all the arancini, make a paste out of the flour plus 1 cup water, and using your hands coat each one with the flour paste. When all have been coated, roll each one in bread crumbs. Refrigerate for at least 1 hour or overnight.

When ready to serve the arancini, deep-fry them in the oil until golden, drain on paper towels, and serve hot or at room temperature.

EGGS

Ova

Modica

Eggs are not a breakfast food in Sicily, but they are considered a very important part of the diet. My mother took great pride in the fact that she, with the help of her father, always managed to get fresh eggs for my brother and myself during World War II. Our grandfather, Don Giovannino Sirugo, would often walk to farms outside of Ragusa to get eggs and milk for us, even braving the perils of bombardments. Since the eggs were super fresh, our mother would make a pinhole on the bottom of the egg, and a larger hole on the top, and we would suck it out. That habit didn't continue after we moved to the Bronx, but our family consumption of eggs was substantial. We had a farmer friend from Hopewell Junction in New Jersey deliver five dozen eggs to our fourth floor walk-up apartment on Willis Avenue while he came to deliver to Vaccaro, the local Italian grocery store on 138th Street.

Our after-school snack would often consist of a frittata made with eggs, chopped garlic, parsley, salt, and pepper, cooked in a little olive oil and enjoyed with a crusty piece of bread. Delicious frittate were often made with leftover vegetables.

I still seek out farm fresh eggs for their superior taste, and like my grandfather, I'm willing to go to the special stores that sell fresh eggs from the Puglisi farm. My husband Howard and I once visited it in South Jersey with our friend Josephine Schinina' Lissandrello, whose uncle Emmanuele Puglisi owns and runs the model farm with his three sons.

EGGS FRIED IN TOMATO SAUCE

Ova fritti ca' sarsa

Serves 1

2 tablespoons extra-virgin olive oil

¼ cup Tomato Sauce (page 80)

2 eggs

Salt and pepper to taste

2 slices crusty bread

Use a small frying pan that can be brought to the table. Heat the olive oil in the pan, add the tomato sauce, and break the eggs into the sauce being careful not to break the yolks. Cover the pan, and allow the eggs to cook to desired doneness. I love them with a runny yolk, but you can hard cook them if you prefer. Season with salt and pepper. Serve with bread to soak up the delicious sauce.

FRITTATA WITH ONIONS AND POTATOES

Frittata ca' cippuda e i patati

Serves 4

I have a frittata pan that I bought in Italy that you just turn to cook the other side. The next time you travel there, treat yourself to one, or better yet to two, in different sizes.

6 tablespoons extra-virgin olive oil

2 potatoes, peeled and cubed

2 onions, sliced

6 eggs

Salt and black pepper to taste

Heat 2 tablespoons of the olive oil in a medium frying pan, and fry the cubed potatoes until they are golden brown. Place in a bowl, and set aside. Add another 2 tablespoons of olive oil to the same pan, and cook the onions until browned and fragrant. Add to the potatoes. Heat the last 2 tablespoons of olive oil in the frying pan, or in a frittata pan if you have one.

Meanwhile, in another bowl, beat the eggs with the salt and pepper, stir in the potatoes and the onions. Pour the mixture in the heated pan, and running a fork along the bottom of the frittata, pierce it, allowing the egg to run to the bottom. When the top is just dry, turn the frittata on to a plate, and slip in back into the frying pan to cook the other side.

SPRING FRITTATA
Frittata cu priselli, cipudda e carcioufuli

Serves 4

4 tablespoons extra-virgin olive oil

2 cloves garlic, chopped

2 tablespoons chopped Italian flat-leaf parsley

1 (10-ounce) package frozen artichoke hearts

5 ounces (½ package) frozen tender tiny peas

Salt and black pepper to taste

6 eggs

Salt and black pepper to taste

Thaw the peas, and the artichokes, and set aside. Cook the garlic in 2 tablespoons of the olive oil until delicately browned. Add the artichokes, and cook for 5 minutes. Add the peas together with the salt and pepper, stir to flavor the peas, and remove from the heat.

In a bowl, beat the eggs, stir in the cooked vegetables and proceed as on page 23 to make into a frittata.

FRITTATA WITH BROCCOLI RAPE
Frittata ri bruocculi rapi

Serves 4 to 6

2 tablespoons olive oil

½ recipe Sautéed Broccoli Rape (page 110), drained of its liquids

6 eggs

Heat the olive oil in a frying pan or in a frittata pan. Meanwhile, beat the eggs, add the broccoli rape, and mix to combine. Proceed to make the frittata as directed on page 23.

EGG AND POTATO STEW

Spizzatinu ri patati cu l'ova

Serves 4 to 6

6 medium potatoes

2 cloves garlic, chopped

¼ cup extra-virgin olive oil

10 sprigs flat-leaf Italian parsley, chopped

1 cup tomato sauce

8 eggs

Salt and pepper to taste

Cut each potato into 4 or 5 chunks. Using a low, wide pan that can be brought to the table, sauté the garlic in the olive oil. Add the parsley, stir to combine, and add the tomato sauce and the potatoes. Add enough water to cover plus 2 inches. Simmer until the potatoes are almost done, then break the eggs into the pot, cover, and cook 15 to 20 minutes until the eggs are set. Season to taste with salt and pepper. Serve with warm crusty garlic bread.

POACHED EGGS SICILIAN-STYLE

Ova rutti all'aqua

Serves 2

Since eggs are not eaten for breakfast, this was a favorite Saturday lunch dish that my father, Felice, would often make. Accompanied with a good piece of crusty bread, or even day old bread dipped in the broth, it was our soul food.

4 tablespoons extra-virgin olive oil

1 clove garlic, chopped

1 tablespoon Italian flat leaf parsley, chopped

4 eggs

Salt and pepper to taste

Heat the olive oil in a small frying pan. Add the garlic and fry until it begins to color. Quickly add the parsley, stir, add 1½ cups water, and salt and pepper. Bring to the boil, carefully break the eggs into the water, and cook to desired doneness. My father always made it with runny yolks, which would flow into the broth and enrich it. Serve the eggs and the broth in a soup plate, dip or break bread right in the broth, and eat with a spoon.

Siracusa

BREADS, SNACKS, AND PIZZA

Pani, merende pe' picciriddi, e pizza

Monreale

Bread, which for Sicilians is the most important part of any meal, is only a mixture of flour, yeast, and water. Dough enriched with eggs, oil, butter or lard is the base of all sorts of delectable dishes. It is the skills, thrift, resourcefulness, ingenuity, and creativity of the Sicilian home cook that made it possible for even the poorest people of this beautiful island to survive, thrive, and enjoy delicious food.

After we came to this country in 1950, my mother never understood why anybody would buy white packaged bread, when with the price paid for one loaf you could buy five pounds of flour and make enough delicious homemade bread to feed a family for a full week. That same bread dough, with a little imagination could be turned into baked wonders such as *scaccie*, savory pies filled with whatever is available and in season. Flattened and pan-fried, sprinkled with salt or with sugar, it makes a delectable snack, appetizer, or accompaniment to any meal.

The bread is made from durum wheat, and is crusty and compact in texture. A loaf of bread is treated with reverence. Decorative shaped breads are made for certain holidays. Easter bread, *Pani ri pasqua cu' l'ova* (page 37), is baked with colored hardboiled eggs right in it. Fanciful bread sculptures are made for the feast of Saint Joseph on March 19, a day that is also celebrated as Father's day in Sicily and throughout Italy.

Pizza is also very popular and is made with some interesting toppings. It's not unusual to find fresh peas on top of a pizza, or as in the classic *sfinciuni palermitano*, toasted bread crumbs for an unexpectedly delicious flavor.

When my brother Carmelo and I came home from school there would always be a *merenda*, an after-school snack that we would often enjoy with a playmate. Of course, we didn't have sandwiches when I was growing up in Sicily; instead we would have a slice of bread with a sweet or savory topping. There was one period shortly after my father returned to Ragusa after the war ended in 1945, at a time when food shortages were still being felt, when he was able to procure a restaurant-size can of orange marmalade. My brother and I enjoyed it thoroughly, but there were times when I was convinced that the marmalade would last for the rest of our lives!

More often than not, our *merenda* would consist of *pani e cumpanagghiu*, a piece of bread in one hand and something "to accompany it" in the other. The *cumpanagghiu* could be cheese, a piece of dried sausage, olives, a piece of fruit or even a piece of chocolate. When I was a student, I would often walk from Hunter College on 68th Street and Park Avenue to New York City's Central Park, my favorite place to read my assignments, while eating a soft, salted pretzel and a bar of chocolate. I even introduced my dear friend and Hunter classmate Eileen White to this very affordable treat that we would enjoy while walking together to the park. I still love this super-deluxe snack.

A good slice of Italian bread drizzled with olive oil and sprinkled with salt is still a favorite snack at anytime of the day.

Bread, in all of its forms, is truly the staff of life for Sicilians. Bread is the favored and most basic of all foods, and it is enjoyed at each and every meal.

Erice

DOUGH FOR ROLLS AND FLAT BREADS

Pasta pe' cuddureddi

Enough for 1 loaf or 16 rolls

3¼ cups unbleached flour

1 tablespoon instant yeast (see page 7)

1 teaspoon salt

¼ cup extra-virgin olive oil

Mix the flour and the yeast in the bowl of a mixed equipped with a dough hook. Add the salt, olive oil, and 1 cup warm water. Mix slowly for 6 minutes. If mixing by hand, place the flour, yeast, and salt in a large bowl. Make a well in the middle, add the water and the oil, and mix with your hands to incorporate the dry ingredients into the liquids. Turn the dough onto a floured surface, and knead for 5 to 10 minutes until smooth and elastic. Put in a lightly oiled bowl, turn the dough to coat all sides with oil, cover, and let rise in a warm place for 1 hour until doubled.

BAKED FLAT BREAD

Matalugghia 'nfurnata

Serves 8

1 recipe Dough for Rolls and Flat Breads (above)

1 beaten egg white

2 tablespoons sesame seeds

Pat and stretch the dough in an oiled or sprayed rectangular jelly-roll pan. Brush the surface with lightly beaten egg white, and sprinkle with sesame seeds. Let rise for 45 minutes. Preheat oven to 375 degrees. Bake for 30 minutes.

FRIED BREAD

Matalugghia fritta

Makes 16

For something so simple, this is absolutely delicious.

1 recipe Dough for Rolls and Flat Breads (page 30)

¼ cup canola or other vegetable oil

Coarse kosher salt to sprinkle on top

Divide the dough in half, and cut each portion into 8 pieces. Roll each piece into a ball, and when all 16 have been shaped, heat the oil in a large frying pan, flatten each ball of dough into a circle and stretch it with your hands. Place them in the frying pan as you flatten each one. Fry them in the hot oil until lightly golden on both sides. Place them on paper towels to absorb any surface oil. Sprinkle with coarse kosher salt, and serve.

FRIED BREAD SLICES

Feddi ri pani fritti

Serves 4 to 6

1 Italian bread, homemade or store-bought, cut into thick slices

½ cup canola oil

Heat the oil in a large frying pan, add the slices in a single layer, and fry until golden brown. Turn each slice and brown the other side. Drain on paper towels.

Variation

SWEET FRIED BREAD SLICES

Feddi ri pani fritti co' zuccuru

Serves 4 to 6

Serve with a dusting of sugar as a snack or as a dessert.

BREAD WITH JAM
Pani ca' marmellata

Serves 2 to 4

4 slices Italian bread

4 teaspoons homemade Quince Jam (below)

Toast the bread, spread with jam, and serve.

QUINCE JAM
Cutugnata

Makes three to four 8-ounce jars or six to eight 4-ounce jars

Quince is very rich in pectin, the substance that allows jams and jellies to thicken or jell. Sugar also acts as a jelling agent and a preservative.

In Sicily, quince jam is cooked until very thick, stirring constantly, and is molded in specially made decorative clay molds. The molds can have a design, or a message such as Buon Anno, which means Happy New Year. When the jam is cold, it's unmolded, placed on a tray, and allowed to air dry. It is then eaten like candy. The most beautiful molds come from the hill town of Caltagirone, a city that has a famous school of ceramic art, a wonderful museum, and hundreds of ceramic studios that welcome visitors.

2 pounds quince

3 to 4 cups sugar

Wash the quince, quarter place in a pot, and add 1 cup of water. Cook over low heat until soft. Put the fruit through a food mill to mash and to remove the cores and the seeds. Measure the fruit, pour into a large pot, and add an equal amount of sugar. Cook over low heat for about 30 minutes, stirring often.

When the jam thickens and turns pink, turn the heat off, and ladle it into 4 or 8-ounce sterilized jars (boiled for 10 minutes) filling them to within 1/2 inch of the top. Place a new lid on each jar, and screw the cap on tightly. Turn each jar upside down as you fill and close them, and 5 minutes after you have inverted the last jar, turn them all right side up.

BREAD WITH SUGAR

Pani co' zuccuru

Serves 2 to 4

2 hard rolls

4 tablespoons unsalted butter, at room temperature

4 teaspoons sugar

Cut the rolls in half as if to make a sandwich. Spread each of the four halves with butter and sprinkle with sugar so that the sugar sticks to the butter. Cut each piece in half.

BREAD WITH OIL

Pani cu' l'uogghiu

Serves 1

Take a thick slice of bread, drizzle it with the best extra-virgin olive oil that you can afford, and drizzle with a little salt.

BREAD AND CHOCOLATE

Pani cu cioccolattu

Serves 1

Take a piece of fresh crusty bread, and take a bite of bread and a bite of chocolate.

SUN-SHAPED BREAD

Throwing ice cubes on the floor of the oven and cooling on a rack, uncovered, makes the bread crusty.

1 recipe Dough for Rolls and Flat Breads (page 30)

1 egg, beaten

Roll dough out into a circle about 15 inches in diameter. Place a soup plate upside down in the middle of the circle. Using a knife or a pair of scissors, cut strips from the edge to the plate all around the circle. Remove the plate, and separate the strips from each other so that the bread looks like the sun. You can then twist the strips if you like. Brush the whole surface with beaten egg. Let rise for 30 minutes. Preheat the oven to 400 degrees. After placing the bread in the oven, throw 5 ice cubes on the floor of the oven, and immediately close the door. Bake for 30 to 40 minutes or until the bread is golden brown. Remove from the oven, and cool on a rack.

HOMEMADE ROLLS

Cuddureddi

Makes 16 rolls

1 recipe Dough for Rolls and Flat Breads (page 30)

1 egg, beaten

Divide the dough into 16 pieces, roll each piece into a ball, place on a greased or sprayed pan about 2 inches apart. Brush with beaten egg, and using a pair of scissors make two parallel cuts on the top of each one. Preheat the oven to 400 degrees. Place the rolls in the oven, toss 5 ice cubes on the floor of the oven, quickly close the door, and bake for 10 to 15 minutes.

CRUSTY BREAD

Pani 'ncrustatu

Serves 6 to 8

I use SAF Gold instant dry yeast. It's added to the flour, and doesn't need to proof. It's good for general bread making, as well as for sweet breads and sourdoughs. It's available through The Baker's Catalogue (see Appendix). Regular yeast can be substituted in equal amounts.

Sponge—Cruscenti

2½ cups flour

1 tablespoon instant yeast

1½ cups warm tap water

Bread Dough—Pasta ri pani

5½ cups unbleached flour

1 tablespoon instant yeast

Mix all sponge ingredients, cover, and let rise overnight at room temperature.

To make the bread: Stir 2 cups warm water into the sponge. Place the flour and instant yeast in the bowl of your mixer, add the sponge mixture, and using the dough hook, mix at slow speed for 6 minutes.

To make the dough by hand, place the flour instant yeast into a large bowl, add the sponge mixed with 2 cups warm water, and mix with your hands until all the flour has been incorporated into the sponge. Turn the dough on to a floured surface, and knead for 6 minutes until smooth and elastic.

Transfer dough to a lightly oiled bowl, turn it in the bowl so that the whole surface is coated with oil, cover and let rise until doubled, about 60 minutes. After the first rising, cover the dough, place in a cool spot or in the refrigerator, and let rest overnight.

When ready to bake the bread, bring the dough to room temperature, and let rise for 1 hour. Divide the dough in half, and gently shape into 2 rounds by smoothing the top and folding it on the bottom. Place the loaves on a lightly oiled baking pan, cover, and let rise for another hour. If you wish to make only 1 loaf, the remaining piece of dough can be refrigerated for 2 to 3 days or frozen for up to 1 month.

Preheat the oven to 400 degrees. Place the bread in the oven, throw 5 ice cubes on the floor of the oven, and quickly close the door. Bake for 60 minutes or until the bread has a lovely brown crust. Remove from the oven, cool on a rack, and hear it crackle and "sing" while it cools!

HOMEMADE SEASONED BREAD

Pani cunzatu fattu 'ncasa

Makes 2 mufulette, each serves 4

My nonna Milina (Carmela Occhipinti Sirugo) made what my husband called Neanderthal bread. It was a very dense Sicilian bread, sometimes oddly shaped, that was delicious and made to last one week. She let the dough rise only once, then she shaped the bread, and baked it after a 30-minute rest. On baking day, she would take one of the smaller loaves out of the oven, cut it in half, and make it cunzatu with the addition of whatever sliced cheese she had in the house. She served it to my husband during a period when he was an art director for the Bergen Record, and worked in Hackensack near her house in Bergenfield, New Jersey.

Covering the bread with a towel after baking softens the crust.

½ recipe Crusty Bread (page 35)

8 tablespoons extra-virgin olive oil

Salt, red pepper flakes, and oregano to taste

Slices of your favorite cheese (optional)

Use the dough immediately after the first rising, or rest in the refrigerator overnight and bring to room temperature before shaping into loaves. Divide the piece of dough in half, dust each piece with flour, and shape each into a *mufuletta*, which is a flattened round. Let rest for 15 minutes while you preheat the oven.

When ready to bake, preheat the oven to 400 degrees. Bake for 20 to 30 minutes or until lightly browned. Remove the 2 loaves from the oven, cover with a towel, and let cool for 15 minutes. Cut the breads in half, lengthwise, drizzle each with 4 tablespoons olive oil, sprinkle with salt, pepper, and just a touch of oregano. Add a few slices of provolone, caciocavallo, mozzarella, or any other cheese you like. Cover with a terrycloth towel, and allow it to cool slowly.

EASTER BREAD WITH EGGS

Pani ri pasqua cu' l'ova

Serves 8 to 10

This recipe makes enough dough for 2 large wreaths. My grandmother Concettina Biazzo Bellia would always make individual little breads, each with 1 egg, for the children. You can do that with half the dough, or save it for another use.

6 cups flour

¼ cup sugar

1 teaspoon salt

2 tablespoons instant yeast (see page 7)

¼ cup vegetable oil

4 raw eggs

8 hard-boiled eggs, tinted with food color

Place the flour, sugar, salt, and yeast into the bowl of a mixer equipped with a dough hook. Add 1½ cups warm water, oil, and 3 raw eggs. Mix and then knead with the dough hook for 5 minutes. Remove from the mixer, give it a few turns, and shape into a ball. Coat with a little oil, and cover with a large inverted bowl to rise until doubled about 1½ hours. Divide the dough in half, and freeze one portion for future use.

Preheat the oven to 375 degrees. Divide the piece of dough into 3 portions, roll each into a 24-inch rope, braid the 3 ropes, and join the ends to form a wreath. Brush with the remaining beaten egg. Tuck the colored eggs into the dough around the top of the wreath, and bake for 45 minutes.

SAUSAGE AND RICOTTA-FILLED ROLLS

Tomasini ri Muorica

Makes 16 filled rolls

This is a favorite picnic food since it's delicious both hot and cold. Lard is used for added flavor, and it's not any less healthful than butter. If you prefer to use butter it'll be just as good.

Tomasini Dough –
   Pasta pe' tomasini

½ cup lard

½ cup shortening

6 cups flour

4 eggs

Filling – Ripienu

2 pounds ricotta cheese

1½ pounds Italian sausage

1 egg, beaten

Work the lard and the shortening into the flour, then add the eggs and ½ cup water. Knead until you have a smooth and pliable dough. Do this by hand or use a mixer with a dough hook. Shape the dough into a ball, cover, and let rest for 1 hour.

Preheat the oven to 400 degrees. Divide the dough into 2 portions, and, working with one piece at a time, roll out thinly into a rectangle about 10 by 12 inches. Take half of the ricotta, and distribute it all over the dough by teaspoonfuls. Take half of the sausage out of its casing, and distribute it in little piles all over the dough next to the ricotta. Starting on the long side, roll as if you were making a jellyroll, and cut into 1½-inch pieces. Repeat with the rest of the dough, meat, and cheese. Place the pieces cut side down on an oiled pan about 2 inches apart. Brush each roll generously with beaten egg on top and on the sides, and bake for 40 minutes. Serve hot or at room temperature.

FILLED BRAIDED BREAD

Pani 'ntricciatu

Serves 8 to 10

1 recipe Dough for Rolls and Flat Breads (page 30)

2 (10-ounce) packages frozen spinach, thawed

1 onion, thinly sliced

6 tablespoon extra-virgin olive oil

½ cup raisins

½ cup broken walnuts

Salt and red pepper flakes to taste

1 egg, beaten

Preheat the oven to 375 degrees.

Squeeze the thawed spinach dry with your hands. Sauté the onion in 2 tablespoons of olive oil olive oil until lightly browned. Add the spinach, raisins, walnuts, salt, and pepper. Stir-fry for 2 minutes, and set aside.

Roll out the dough into a long rectangle (about 10 by 15 inches) and place on an oiled baking sheet. **1.** Spoon the spinach filling in the middle of the rectangle lengthwise. Drizzle with the remaining 4 tablespoons of olive oil. **2.** Fold the top and the bootom over the spinach. **3.** Cut the dough on either side of the filling in diagonal strips. **4.** Fold the strips over the filling, alternating one from the right and one from the left. Brush with the beaten egg and bake for 1 hour. Remove from the oven, cover with a clean towel and then with a woolen blanket or with a doubled bath towel for 1 to 2 hours or until ready to serve. Serve warm or at room temperature.

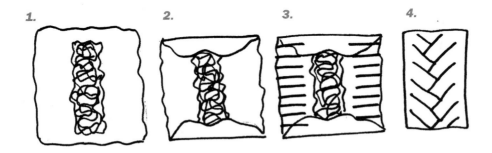

1.   2.   3.   4.

Pizza Basics
PIZZA DOUGH

Pasta pa' pizza
Makes 2 pizzas, each with 12 portions

6½ cups flour

1 tablespoon instant yeast
(see page 7)

¼ cup extra-virgin olive oil

1 teaspoon salt

Mix all ingredients and 2 cups water in a mixer equipped with a dough hook for 3 minutes on low, then 7 minutes on medium. If you don't have a dough hook, knead the dough until smooth and elastic, about 10 minutes. Shape into a ball, place in an oiled bowl, and turn the dough upside down to coat with oil. Cover and let rise until doubled, about 1 hour. Divide in half and stretch each half to fit a well-oiled 11 by 15-inch baking pan. Let rise while preparing the toppings.

FRIED ONIONS

Cipuddi fritti
Enough for 2 pizzas

¼ cup extra-virgin olive oil

4 large onions, sliced

Sprinkle of dried oregano

Heat the olive oil in a large skillet, add the onions and oregano, and cook until the onions begin to color.

SICILIAN PIZZA

Pizza Siciliana

Makes 12 portions

½ recipe Pizza Dough (page 40)

1½ cups Mama' Milina's Spicy Tomato Sauce (page 81)

½ recipe Fried Onions (page 40)

1 (10-ounce) package frozen tiny tender peas, unthawed

¼ cup extra-virgin olive oil

Preheat oven to 400 degrees. Stretch the dough on an oiled 10 by 15-inch pan. Spoon the sauce on the pizza, distribute the onions on top of the sauce, top with the still-frozen peas, and drizzle with olive oil. Bake for 20 to 30 minutes. Serve at room temperature.

PIZZA WITH ANCHOVIES

Pizza c' anciuovi

Makes 12 portions

½ recipe Pizza Dough (page 40)

½ recipe Fried Onions (page 40)

1 (4-ounce) can flat anchovy fillets

½ cup extra-virgin olive oil

Preheat oven to 400 degrees. Stretch the dough on an oiled 10 by 15-inch pan. Spread the fried onions on the pizza, place the anchovy fillets in a diamond pattern, and drizzle with olive oil. Bake for 20 to 30 minutes. Serve at room temperature.

ZUCCHINI PIZZA

Pizza che' cucuzzeddi

Makes 12 portions

½ recipe Pizza Dough (page 40)

2 medium zucchini

½ cup extra-virgin olive oil

4 cloves garlic, chopped

Salt and black pepper to taste

½ cup grated caciocavallo,
  pecorino, or Parmigiano cheese

Peel the zucchini and cut into ½-inch rounds. Fry in ¼ cup of the olive oil until delicately browned on both sides. Set aside.

Preheat oven to 400 degrees. Stretch the dough on an oiled 10 by 15-inch pan. With your fingers, make indentations all over the surface of the dough, sprinkle the garlic all over, drizzle with the remaining ¼ cup olive oil, distribute the zucchini rounds on top of the dough, and top with the salt, pepper and grated cheese. Bake for 30 minutes. Serve hot or cold.

WHITE PIZZA

Pizza ca' ricotta

Makes 12 portions

½ recipe Pizza Dough (page 40)

½ cup extra-virgin olive oil

2 cups ricotta

8 ounces mozzarella cheese,
  shredded

Salt and pepper to taste

Preheat oven to 400 degrees. Stretch the dough on an oiled 10 by 15-inch pan. Distribute the ricotta all over the dough, top with the mozzarella, drizzle with olive oil, and sprinkle with salt and pepper. Bake for 30 minutes.

PIZZA OF PALERMO

Sfinciuni Palermitanu

Serves 6 to 8

I sometimes make this in an electric frying pan set at 350 degrees, and I cook it covered for 30 to 40 minutes. It comes out delicious.

½ recipe Pizza Dough (page 40)

1½ cups Tomato Sauce (page 80)

½ recipe Fried Onions (page 40)

1 cup Toasted Bread Crumbs (page 68)

¼ cup extra-virgin olive oil

Preheat oven to 400 degrees. Stretch the dough into a round 10 to 12-inch deep dish pan. Spoon the sauce on top of the dough, distribute the fried onions over the sauce, sprinkle the bread crumbs on top, and drizzle with the oil. Bake for 30 to 40 minutes. Serve at room temperature.

Palermo

Taormina

SOUPS

Minesre

Ragusa Ibla – San Giorgio – This is a view of the church from the Piazza.

Soups, called *minestre* in Italian and *minesre* in Sicilian, are the mainstay of Sicilian cooking. They are generally very easy to make, economical, comforting, and delicious. These soups are rich in proteins if made with dried beans, refreshing to the stomach if made with vegetables, and nutritious if made with a chicken or meat broth. Combining pasta with beans, vegetables, or broths makes the dish nutritionally complete.

Sicilians buy their fish whole, and since nothing edible is thrown away, marvelous fish soups are made from the heads of the fish that are cooked for the main course. The first time we were in Maine and we went to the fishmonger, I asked if he had any fish heads for soup, to which he answered "But you don't look Italian!" (because I'm tall and light-haired). Sicily had so many invasions during the past two thousand years that we are among the most physically diversified people on the planet.

In soup making, we don't use stocks. The water used is naturally flavored by the ingredients in the soup. The addition of extra-virgin olive oil after the soup is cooked imparts a wonderfully delicious flavor. Although most dishes begin with olive oil, some is nearly always added after cooking, particularly in the case of soups and vegetables. The full flavor of a good olive oil comes through when it is eaten raw. That is why if you really want to taste the flavor of an olive oil, you dip a piece of bread in it and you enjoy the morsel.

CHICKEN BROTH

Bruoru ri iaddina

Makes 2 quarts of broth

Chicken broth is served clear with pastina, fine egg noodles homemade or purchased, or rice. I generally use dried Italian porcini, but any type of dried mushrooms will do. Ricotta and grated cheese are served at the table and are added to the chicken soup according to one's taste. The ricotta makes the chicken soup deliciously creamy.

2 to 3 pounds chicken

10 sprigs fresh Italian flat-leaf parsley with stems (if not available omit)

1 leek

4 dried mushrooms

1 teaspoon black peppercorns

Salt to taste

Bring 10 cups water to the boil. Add the chicken, bring back to the boil, skim the surface, and add parsley, leek, dried mushrooms, peppercorns, and salt. Lower the heat, cover and simmer for 1½ hours or until tender.

Take the chicken out of the broth, cool, and bone. Reserve the chicken meat for another use. Strain the broth, cover, and refrigerate. When ready to use, remove the hardened surface fat, and use for soup.

CHICKEN SOUP WITH TINY MEATBALLS AND EGG NOODLES

Bruoru che' pallottolini e i taghiarini

Serves 4 to 6

Tiny Meatballs – Pallottolini

½ pound ground veal or beef sirloin

1 egg

3 tablespoons grated pecorino, caciocavallo, or Parmigiano cheese

3 tablespoons dried bread crumbs

1 clove garlic, finely chopped

2 tablespoons chopped Italian flat-leaf parsley

Salt and pepper to taste

Soup – Bruoru

6 cups chicken broth (page 47)

8 ounces fine egg noodles

½ cup grated Italian cheese

2 cups ricotta (optional)

Mix all the meatball ingredients and shape into balls the size of marbles. Refrigerate until ready to cook, or freeze for future use.

Bring the broth to the boil. Add the meatballs and the egg noodles, and cook for 3 to 5 minutes. Serve with grated cheese. Pass the ricotta at the table if you wish.

ASPARAGUS SOUP WITH RICE

Minesra ri sparici co' risu

Serves 4 to 6

2 cloves garlic, chopped

¼ cup extra-virgin olive oil

10 sprigs Italian flat-leaf parsley, chopped

1 pound green asparagus or the ends of 2 pounds asparagus

Salt and pepper to taste

¾ cup uncooked rice

½ cup grated Italian cheese

Sauté the garlic in the olive oil, and as it begins to color, add the parsley. Stir, and add the asparagus ends, together with 6 cups of water and the salt and pepper. Bring it to the boil, and simmer for 45 minutes.

Place the stems and some of the liquid in a food processor, liquefy, then put through a sieve or a food mill to remove the fibers. Put the broth back in the pot, bring it to the boil, add the rice and simmer for 15 minutes. Add the cheese, and serve hot.

Note:

If you use the whole asparagus, snap off the tip of each spear, use the rest as directed, and add the tips to the soup 10 minutes after the rice.

BROCCOLI AND RICOTTA SOUP

Minesra ri bruocculi e ricotta

Serves 4 to 6

My husband Howard began eating broccoli only after we were married, and this became one of his favorite soups. His mother May Murray had attended The Boston Cooking School before her marriage to Bill La Marca, but her 1915 Fanny Farmer Cookbook didn't mention broccoli, a vegetable that only Italian immigrants grew for themselves.

1 bunch broccoli

1 recipe Semolina Noodles (below)

1 (15-ounce) container ricotta cheese

Salt and pepper to taste

¼ cup extra-virgin olive oil

Cut the florets from of broccoli and set aside. Trim the broccoli stems and chop. Bring 2 quarts of water to the boil, add the chopped broccoli, and cook for 30 minutes. Add the florets and the noodles, and cook for 5 minutes. Pour into a soup tureen, add the ricotta, salt and pepper, mix to combine, add the olive oil and stir.

SEMOLINA NOODLES

Pasta 'mpastata ri simula

Serves 4

½ cup flour

¼ cup semolina

1 egg

Process the flour, semolina, and egg, adding 1 tablespoonful of water if needed, and processing until the dough becomes a mass. Roll it out thinly using plenty of flour so that the sheet of dough doesn't stick to the surface on which you are working. Roll the sheet of dough as thin as possible, and cut it into 1/4-inch strips. If you have a pasta machine, divide the dough into 4 pieces, roll out each piece medium thick, and cut it into fettuccine. Be sure to use plenty of flour as you roll out and cut the sheets of dough.

PASTA, RICE, RICOTTA, AND CAULIFLOWER SOUP

Pasta, risu, ricotta e scamuzza

Serves 4 to 6

This is a soup that my mother, who was born in 1909, remembered from her childhood. It always amused her to recall that her little brother Nini', unable to pronounce all the words, called it Pacca Ricu Ricocca e Camucca. *Nini', loved it so much that he had to eat it out of his own special (big) bowl, which he called* a scutedda che' patrinosra, *a large bowl with a decorative pattern on the edge that looked to him like rosary beads. Zio Nini', now 83, still has a hearty appetite, and a wonderful sense of humor.*

Scamuzza is a leafy vegetable to which there is no equivalent, but cauliflower has a similar flavor and is a good substitute. Since the ingredients are white, white pepper adds the flavor without the black specks.

½ head cauliflower, separated into florets

½ cup uncooked rice

½ cup uncooked tubettini or any small pasta

Salt and white pepper to taste

2 cups fresh ricotta cheese

¼ cup extra-virgin olive oil

Bring 6 cups of water to the boil. Add the cauliflower, rice, salt, and pepper. Lower the heat, and simmer for 10 minutes. Add the pasta and cook for 10 more minutes. Remove from the heat, add the ricotta, stir to combine, add the olive oil, stir again, and serve.

POTATO SOUP

Pasta che' patati

Serves 4 to 6

6 medium potatoes

4 cloves garlic, chopped

6 tablespoons cup extra-virgin olive oil

4 tablespoons chopped Italian flat-leaf parsley

Salt and pepper to taste

½ cup grated Italian cheese

4 ounces spaghetti, broken into 1-inch pieces

Cube the potatoes and set aside. Sauté the garlic in 3 tablespoons of the olive oil until it barely begins to color. Add the parsley, stir, add the potatoes and stir for 1 minute to blend the flavors. Add 6 cups of water, salt and pepper to taste, and bring to the boil. Lower the heat, and simmer for 30 minutes. Add the pasta, and cook for 10 additional minutes. Turn the heat off, add the grated cheese and the remaining 3 tablespoons olive oil. Stir and serve hot.

ZUCCHINI SOUP

Pasta ca' cucuzzedda

Serves 4 to 6

2 zucchini

2 cloves garlic

¼ cup extra-virgin olive oil

10 sprigs flat-leaf Italian parsley, chopped

1 cup tomato sauce

Salt and pepper to taste

1 cup uncooked small pasta

½ cup grated Italian cheese

Peel the zucchini, wash them, quarter them lengthwise, cut each piece into ½-inch slices, and set aside.

Sauté the garlic in 2 tablespoons of the olive oil, add the parsley, and stir. Add the tomato sauce, salt, and pepper, and 6 cups of water. Bring to the boil, add the zucchini and the pasta, lower the heat, and simmer for 10 minutes. Remove from the heat, add the cheese, and drizzle with the remaining 2 tablespoons of olive oil.

EGG AND ZUCCHINI SOUP

Pasta cu' ova e cucuzzeddi

Serves 4 to 6

¼ cup extra-virgin olive oil

2 cloves garlic, chopped

2 tablespoons chopped Italian flat-leaf parsley

2 zucchini, cut into small cubes

¾ cup uncooked ditalini or your favorite small pasta

2 eggs

Salt and black pepper to taste

½ cup grated pecorino or Parmigiano cheese

Heat the olive oil in a saucepan, add the garlic, and as it barely begins to color, add the parsley. Stir, add 6 cups of water, and bring to the boil. Add the zucchini and cook for 10 minutes. Add the pasta and cook for 7 minutes. Break the unbeaten eggs into the soup and stir wit a fork to make egg shreds. Turn off the heat. Salt and pepper to taste. Add the grated cheese, stir, and serve.

VEGETABLE SOUP

Minesra ri virdura

Makes 12 servings

For variety, ladle the soup over a piece of grilled, toasted, or fried bread, and enjoy with a drizzle of olive oil. This soup is good either hot or at room temperature.

2 onions, chopped

6 tablespoons extra-virgin olive oil

2 carrots, chopped

2 stalks celery with leaves, chopped

2 potatoes, cubed

¼ head cabbage, shredded

1 cup tomato sauce or tomato puree

2 zucchini, quartered and sliced

1 cup uncooked pasta

Salt and pepper to taste

¼ cup grated cheese

Sauté the onions in 2 tablespoons of the olive oil. Add the carrots, celery, potatoes, cabbage, and tomato sauce. Add 10 cups of water, bring to the boil, cover, and simmer over low heat for 1 hour. Add the zucchini, together with the pasta. Cook 10 minutes, then add the salt, pepper, and cheese, and drizzle with the remaining 4 tablespoons olive oil.

CHICKPEA SOUP

Pasta che' ciciri

Serves 4 to 6

In 1282, during the violent revolt known as the Sicilian Vespers (immortalized by composer Giuseppe Verdi in his opera I Vespri Siciliani)*, the French, who were the oppressors, were tested by their pronunciation of* ciciri. *If a person could not pronounce the word as a Sicilian native would by rolling the "r," which the French were not able to do, that person became the next victim. The power of words!*

Broth from Chickpeas with Fennel (page 118)

1 recipe Processor Pastina (page 65) or 1 cup small pasta such as tubettini or ditalini

¼ cup extra-virgin olive oil

Salt and pepper to taste

Bring the broth with any leftover chickpeas and fennel to the boil. Add the processor pasta, whisk to separate the granules, and cook for 5 minutes. If using dried pasta, cook for 7 to 10 minutes. Pour into a soup tureen, add olive oil and salt and pepper to taste, and serve.

LENTIL SOUP

My mother Concettina broke homemade, day-old Italian bread into this soup, and seasoned it with additional extra-virgin olive oil and red pepper flakes.

Broth from Lentils with Broccoli
(page 119)

1 bunch broccoli, stems and
leaves only, chopped

½ recipe fresh Broad Egg
Noodles (page 64) or coarse
Processor Pastina (page 65)

¼ cup extra-virgin olive oil

Salt to taste

Red pepper flakes to taste
(optional)

Slices of day-old or toasted Italian
bread (optional)

Bring the lentil broth to the boil. Add the broccoli stems and leaves, return to the boil, and simmer for 30 minutes. Add the pasta, and cook until it comes to the surface. Add the olive oil, salt, and red pepper flakes to taste. If you want a thicker soup, add additional lentils and broccoli. Serve hot with bread if desired.

BEAN SOUP

Minesra ri casola co' risu

Serves 6 to 8

This soup too is delicious with bread broken into it topped with an extra drizzle of extra-virgin olive oil and red pepper flakes.

Broth from Beans with Celery (page 120)

1 cup uncooked Italian arborio or American Carolina rice

¼ cup extra-virgin olive oil

Salt and pepper to taste

Slices of day-old Italian bread (optional)

Red pepper flakes (optional)

Bring the bean broth to the boil. Add the rice and cook for 20 minutes. Turn off the heat, ladle into a soup tureen, and add the olive oil, salt, and pepper to taste. If you want a thicker soup, you can add additional cooked beans. Serve hot with bread and red pepper flakes if desired.

FAVA BEAN PUREE

Maccu ri favi

Serves 6 to 8

Purists like their maccu *plain. In my hometown of Ragusa, it's such a favorite dish that we are often called* Rausani mangia maccu, *or* Ragusani, *the eaters of* maccu.

Fava beans must soak overnight, so plan ahead.

---

1 pound dried whole or dried split and skinned fava beans, soaked overnight

¼ cup extra-virgin olive oil

Salt and pepper to taste

Fried Bread Slices (page 31) or cooked tubettini pasta (optional)

Drain the soaked fava beans, rinse, and drain again. If using whole beans, slip the skins off. Place beans in a heavy bottomed pot, add 6 cups cold water, and bring to the boil. Lower the heat to simmer, cover, and cook for 1 to 1½ hours or until they can be crushed with a fork against the side of the pot, and have melted into the soup, making it smooth and velvety. Stir the pot often to be sure that nothing is sticking. If it becomes too thick, add a cup of boiling water.

Turn the heat off, and use a portable blender to make a smooth puree right in the pot, or you can put the soup through a food mill, or in a food processor. Pour into a soup tureen, season with olive oil, salt and pepper to taste. Serve plain, or over fried bread slices, or with cooked pasta if desired.

FISH BROTH

*Try to use a variety of fish heads or any of the less expensive fish.
You can even make a fish broth using the shells of two pounds of
shrimp; nothing is wasted!*

¼ cup extra-virgin olive oil

2 cloves garlic

2 tablespoons chopped Italian
flat-leaf parsley

½ cup tomato sauce or tomato
puree

2 pounds fish heads

Salt and black pepper to taste

Heat the olive oil, add the garlic and sauté until it barely begins to color. Add the parsley, stir, then add the tomato sauce, the fish heads, and enough water to cover plus 2 inches (about 8½ cups). Add salt and black pepper to taste, bring to the boil, lower the heat, cover, and simmer for 30 minutes. Strain, and if you've used heads you can simply throw them away. If you've used fish, bone it and serve as a salad.

FISH SOUP WITH RICE

6 cups Fish Broth (above)

¾ cup uncooked rice

Salt and pepper to taste

Bring the broth to the boil, add the rice, and bring it back to the boil. Lower the heat, cover, and simmer for 20 minutes. Adjust the salt and pepper before serving.

Segesta – closeup of Temple

PASTA DISHES
Pastasciutta

Pasta in all of its wonderful varieties is nutritious, filling, and satisfying like no other food The presentation and the fragrance of an elaborate pasta dish will evoke thrills of joy. Yet *Pasta cu' l'agghiu e l'uogghiu*, in its absolute simplicity and ease of preparation can be truly called fast food, and it is as delicious as any of its more elaborate cousins. *Pasta che sardi* is a classic dish of Sicilian cuisine with its topping of toasted bread crumbs rather than cheese. Made just with anchovies and toasted bread crumbs it's delicious and can be prepared in a flash. Delectable *Pasta alla Norma* honors the great Bel Canto composer Vincenzo Bellini, who was born in Catania, Sicily, and whose opera *Norma* gives the dish its name. The *Timballo* is a truly princely dish rich, fragrant, and delicious recalling one of the many parties given by the prince of Salina in the book *Il Gattopardo* (The Leopard), which

Giardini Naxos – Monument commemorating the landing of the Greeks in Sicily in 735 B.C. when they first colonized the island.

became an instant best seller immediately after its publication in 1957. This was the first published of a scholarly Sicilian aristocrat, Giuseppe Tomasi di Lampedusa, who was a brilliant twentieth-century writer, as well as a prince and a gourmet.

Causunedda, dense, chewy handmade noodles, are so easy and quick to make that you will want to enlist the help of the children in the family in shaping them. It was one of the first things my grandmother Concettina allowed me to make with her. For a quick treat we would make a small portion, while the cooking water was brought to the boil. We would make the noodles very big, then simply boil them in salted water, and season them with olive oil, red pepper flakes, and plenty of grated cheese. The thought of this country-style dish still makes me hungry for it!

HOMEMADE PASTA

3 cups flour

4 eggs

1 teaspoon extra-virgin olive oil

To make by hand: Place the flour on a clean surface, make a well in the middle, break the eggs into the flour, and beat while beginning to incorporate some of the flour. If necessary add a little water to mix all the flour into a soft dough. Working on a floured surface so it doesn't stick, and knead it for 5 minutes into a smooth dough. Shape the dough into a ball, coat it with a little oil, cover it with a bowl, and let it rest for 30 minutes.

To make in the food processor: Place the flour in the food processor, add the eggs and process. If the dough does not form a mass, add water 1 tablespoon at a time until becomes a solid mass. Take it out of the processor, knead it a few turns until smooth. Shape into a ball, coat it with a little oil, cover it with a bowl, and let it rest for 30 minutes.

Please refer to specific recipes for rolling, shaping, and cooking instructions.

BROAD AND FINE EGG NOODLES

Lasagneddi e taghiarini

Serves 4 to 6 people cut wide, 6 to 8 cut fine for soup

1 recipe Homemade Pasta for broad noodles or ½ for fine noodles

To cut by hand: Cut the dough in half, shape each portion into a ball, and work with one piece at a time on a well-floured surface. Roll it out with a rolling pin sprinkling it with flour as you roll it, until it's as thin as possible. Making sure that both the top and the bottom of the dough are well floured, roll it loosely in jelly-roll fashion, and cut into little ribbons. As you cut them, loosen them into long strands and place on a towel until ready to cook. Usually, if the pasta ribbons are cut wide (*Lasagneddi*) they will be served with sauce; if they are cut as thin as possible (*Taghiarini*), they will be cooked in broth.

To cut using a pasta machine: Cut the dough into 8 pieces, and feed each well-floured piece into the pasta machine, rolling the pieces thinner and thinner each time you put them through. As you finish rolling out each piece, hang them on dowels that you might place on the backs of chairs, to dry. When all the pasta has been rolled out, cut each strip to the length you wish, and put through the cutter of the pasta machine. As you cut them, loosen the strands, and place them on a towel until ready to cook.

To cook: Drop the desired amount of *lasagneddi* (wide egg noodles) into boiling water or *taghiarini* (fine egg noodles) into boiling broth, or soup and cook only until the pasta comes to the surface.

PROCESSOR PASTINA

Pastina minuta minuta

Serves 6 to 8

1½ cups flour

2 eggs

1 tablespoon flour

Place the flour in the food processor, add the eggs and process. If the dough becomes a solid mass, add 1 tablespoon of flour as you pulse to make the granules of pasta. If the dough does not form a mass, add 1 tablespoon of water, and when it does become a solid mass, add a table-spoon of flour and proceed as described above. Make the pastina while the soup or broth is boiling, and as soon as it does boil, add the pastina all at once, and stir with a whisk to separate the pasta granules. Cook for 2 minutes or until it comes to the surface.

HANDMADE PASTA

Causunedda

Serves 6 to 8 in soup and 4 to 6 with sauce

Make the homemade pasta on page 63, divide the dough in half, and roll out each piece into a sheet about ¼ inch thick on a well-floured board. Cut the sheet into ¾ -inch strips, and cut each strip into ½ -inch pieces. Holding a fork in your left hand, take each little piece of dough, and press into the tines of the fork with the index and middle finger of the right hand. Lightly press and roll each piece forward to form a ridged piece of pasta. This is easy to do and very quick, get someone to help you and you'll both have fun. Drop into boiling soup or into boiling salted water if serving with sauce. Cook for 7 to 10 minutes.

SPAGHETTI WITH BROCCOLI RAPE

Spaghetti che' bruocculi rapi

Serves 6 to 8

¼ cup extra-virgin olive oil

Red pepper flakes to taste

4 cloves garlic, chopped

1 pound spaghetti, cooked

½ cup spaghetti cooking water

1 to 2 cups Sautéed Broccoli Rape (page 110)

½ cup grated caciocavallo or Romano cheese

Heat the olive oil in a large skillet, add the red pepper flakes and the garlic. When the garlic barely begins to brown, add the cooked spaghetti together with the cooking liquid. Add the broccoli rape, and the cheese. Mix well, pour onto a serving platter, and serve hot or at room temperature.

SPAGHETTI WITH GARLIC AND OIL

Pasta cu l'agghiu e l'uogghiu

Serves 6 to 8

I like to top pasta and vegetables with a generous drizzle of extra-virgin olive oil just before serving. The best flavor of the olive oil is retained when the oil is not heated, so although olive oil is used in cooking, a little raw olive oil makes a dish more delicious.

1 pound uncooked spaghetti

⅓ to ½ cup extra-virgin olive oil

4 cloves garlic, chopped

Red pepper flakes to taste

½ cup grated sharp cheese such as caciocavallo, provolone, or Romano

Bring a pot of water to the boil. Add the spaghetti, stir, cover to quickly bring the water back to the boil, remove the cover, lower the heat and cook for 7 to 10 minutes. The pasta should be al dente; be careful not to overcook. Reserve ½ cup of the cooking water before you drain the pasta.

While the pasta is cooking, heat the olive oil, and add the garlic and the red pepper flakes so that both ingredients release their fragrance. Just as the garlic begins to color, turn off the heat to keep it from burning, add the drained spaghetti, and the reserved pasta cooking water. Toss the spaghetti in the oil, add the grated cheese, mix, and serve immediately.

LINGUINE WITH ANCHOVIES

Pasta c'anciuovi
Serves 6 to 8

1 pound uncooked linguine

½ cup extra-virgin olive oil

4 cloves garlic

Red pepper flakes to taste

1 (4-ounce) can flat anchovy fillets

1 cup Toasted Bread Crumbs (below)

Cook the linguine in boiling water until al dente, 7 to 10 minutes. Drain, reserving ½ cup cooking water.

Meanwhile, heat the olive oil, add the garlic and the red pepper flakes, and cook for 1 minute. Add the anchovies, and let them melt into the oil. Add the drained linguine and the reserved pasta cooking water. Toss and let stand for 2 minutes. Place on a serving platter, top with some of the toasted bread crumbs, and quickly bring to the table. Pass the rest of the toasted bread crumbs at the table.

TOASTED BREAD CRUMBS

Pani rattatu abbrustulitu
Makes 1 cup

1 cup plain dried bread crumbs (not the flavored variety)

2 tablespoons extra-virgin olive oil

Place the bread crumbs in a small frying pan, add the olive oil, mix it well, and stir over low heat until the bread crumbs are delicately browned. Immediately remove them from the pan, as they burn easily at this point.

PENNE WITH CAULIFLOWER

Pinni che' sciuriddi
Serves 6 to 8

1 head cauliflower

1 tablespoon salt

1 pound uncooked penne pasta

4 cloves garlic

½ cup extra-virgin olive oil

1 (2-ounce) can flat anchovy fillets

⅓ cup pignoli (pine nuts)

⅓ cup raisins

¼ to ½ teaspoon red pepper flakes

Wash and separate the cauliflower into small florets. Bring 4 cups water and the salt to the boil. Add the cauliflower, cook for 10 minutes and remove to a bowl with a skimmer. Cook the pasta in the same water. Reserve ½ cup of the cooking water, and drain.

While the penne are cooking, sauté the garlic and the red pepper flakes in the olive oil. Add the anchovies, and stir until they melt into the oil. Add the pignoli and raisins, mix, add the reserved pasta cooking water and the cooked cauliflower. Turn the heat off until you are ready to add the cooked pasta.

Place the pan on low heat, add the pasta, toss well to mix the flavors, and serve with Toasted Bread Crumbs (page 68) for each guest to add at the table.

PASTA WITH FENNEL AND SARDINES

Pasta che' sardi

Serves 6 to 8

Most Italian grocery stores carry Cuoco's seasoning for macaroni with sardines, or condimento per pasta con sarde, which is quite good. I use this ready-made sauce when I can't find fresh sardines. I still follow this recipe, omitting the fennel and the sardines since both ingredients are already in the sauce. I do add the additional raisins and pine nuts for a richer flavor.

Feathery leaves from 2 fennel bulbs or 2 large bunches of fresh dill

½ cup extra-virgin olive oil

1 pound cleaned fresh sardines or 2 (6-ounce) cans of sardines

4 cloves garlic, chopped

1 (4-ounce) can flat anchovy fillets

½ cup raisins

½ cup pignoli (pine nuts)

1 pound bucatini or perciatelli pasta

Wash the fennel leaves and remove the tough stems and any discolored leaves. Cook in 8 cups boiling salted water for 10 minutes or until tender but still bright green. Remove the fennel from the water with a slotted spoon, cool, chop coarsely, and set aside.

Meanwhile, clean, trim, wash, and towel dry the sardines. Heat the olive oil, add the sardines, and fry until golden brown on both sides (about 5 minutes). Without turning off the heat, remove the sardines from the pan, leave the oil in the pan, and set aside.

Add the garlic to the leftover oil, stir, and before the garlic begins to color, add the anchovy fillets, and let them dissolve into the oil. Add the raisins, pignoli, cooked fennel and half of the fried sardines, reserving the nicest looking ones to top the pasta. If using canned sardines, simply add them to the sauce. Cook 5 minutes, and turn the heat off. Cook the pasta in the fennel water, drain, and reserve ½ cup of the cooking water. Add the drained pasta to the sauce together with the reserved pasta water. Toss well. Place on a serving platter, arrange the rest of the fried sardines on top, and serve with Toasted Bread Crumbs (page 68), which will be passed around at the table.

PASTA WITH EGGPLANT

Pasta alla Norma

Serves 6 to 8

Brush or spray the eggplant slices with olive oil, and grill or broil them, but the very best flavor comes by frying them in oil. I like to fry them in vegetable oil rather than in olive oil, but you can do either.

2 eggplants

Kosher salt

½ to 1 cup canola or other vegetable oil

1 pound uncooked spaghetti or macaroni

2 cups Mama Milina's Spicy Tomato Sauce (page 81)

8 ounces ricotta salata, shredded or Greek feta cheese, crumbled

Cut the eggplants lengthwise into ½-inch slices. Layer them in a colander sprinkling salt in between the layers. Top the stack of slices with a weight (I use a water-filled tea kettle) and let them drain off the dark bitter juices for at least 30 minutes. When ready to fry them, rinse off the salt, dry on paper towels, and fry in the hot oil.

Cook the pasta according to the package directions. Drain, place in a bowl, add the sauce and the cheese, reserving some of each for the topping. Arrange the fried eggplant all around the serving platter allowing the slices to hang over the edge. Spoon the pasta into the serving platter, fold the eggplant slices over the pasta, top with the reserved sauce and serve hot or at room temperature.

MOLDED MACARONI

Timballu ri pasta

Serves 8 to 12

This is a very rich dish, so a small portion is quite adequate as a first course or as part of a buffet.

2 to 3 sheets puff pastry

1 pound uncooked bucatini or perciatelli

4 cups Sauce with Meatballs and Sausage (page 83)

2 cups meat from Sauce with Meatballs and Sausage (page 83)

1 pound mozzarella, cubed

1 cup grated Italian cheese

1 (10-ounce) package frozen tiny tender peas, thawed

1 egg, beaten

½ cup heavy cream (optional)

Line the bottom and sides of a 9½-inch spring-form pan with puff pastry, allowing it to over-hang the top of the pan. Cut and piece the pastry as necessary to completely line the pan. Keep it cool while you prepare the filling.

Cook the pasta just until limp because it will continue to cook in the oven. Drain it well, reserving ½ cup cooking water, and place it in a large bowl.

Preheat oven to 375 degrees. Add 2 cups of sauce to the drained pasta and mix well. Add the meat, mozzarella, grated cheese, and peas, and mix to distribute everything. Pour the pasta mixture in the pastry-lined pan. Place a circle of puff pastry on top, and flip the overhanging pastry over the circle. Brush with egg, and bake for 1 hour. Let rest for 1 hour before cutting into wedges.

Serve with the remaining 2 cups sauce mixed with the cream. If you don't wish to thin the sauce with cream, simply add ½ cup of the pasta cooking water.

RAVIOLI FROM RAGUSA

Ravioli Rausani

Serves 4

The ravioli made in Ragusa are unique in that they have a sweet filling, but they are topped with a flavorful meat sauce. I warn you that they are addictive!

2 cups fresh ricotta cheese

2 tablespoons of sugar

Grated peel of 1 orange

½ recipe Homemade Pasta (page 63)

Place the ricotta in a colander lined with damp cheesecloth, and refrigerate for 2 hours. Mix the drained ricotta, sugar, and grated peel. Roll out dough by hand, on a counter, as thinly as possible, or use a pasta machine set to the next to the thinnest setting. Place heaping teaspoonfuls of ricotta filling 2 inches apart on the long side of the dough about 1 inch from the edge. Fold the dough over the ricotta filling, and press the dough around the filling. Using a pastry wheel, cut the ravioli apart in squares and press the edges carefully to be sure that they are sealed. Place the ravioli on a cookie sheet covered with a towel sprinkled with a little flour so that the fresh ravioli don't stick.

When ready to cook the ravioli, drop them into boiling salted water. When they float on the surface they are done. Top with Meat Sauce (page 82), Sauce with Meatballs and Sausage (page 83), or Sunday Meat Sauce (page 84).

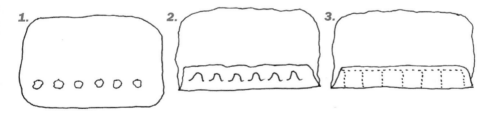

1. *Roll out sheet of dough*
2. *Place ricotta filling along the bottom edge*
3. *Fold the dough over the filling, and cut with a pastry wheel*

Ragusa Ibla from Santa Maria delle Scale – This church stands halfway between Ragusa and Ragusa Ibla. Ragusa is built on a mountain, and Ragusa Ibla is on a smaller mountain below Ragusa. The two sections of the city are connected by a series of staircases, and as you descend you see beautiful panoramas of the ancient part of the city that is Ragusa Ibla.

SAUCES

Sarsi

Ragusa Ibla – Panorama

People are often surprised to find that many sauces in Sicilian cooking don't include tomato. These sauces are called *in bianco*, fish-based sauces are made both with fresh fish and with canned tuna. As anyone who has been to Italy and to Sicily may remember, they are adamant about not serving grated cheese with a fish sauce even though many Americans have become used to sprinkling grated cheese on anything that is Italian. Traditionally, Toasted Bread Crumbs (page 68) are passed around at the table to top pasta with a fish sauce.

Some of the sauces are not even cooked, so they are easy and very quick to make and they bring the fragrance and the taste of ripe ingredients enhanced by nothing more than good extra-virgin olive oil, lemon juice, and a sprinkle of salt. I cannot say enough about the importance of using the best extra-virgin olive oil you can afford, since that is where the flavor is.

My godmother Tina Cannizzaro Distefano, who is a talented and creative cook, splashes swordfish steaks with *salmurigliu* immediately after her husband Meno takes them off the grill. This simple sauce sparks the flavor of fish and even meats with its lemony tang and fruity olive oil.

A rich and delicious *ragu'* made with a variety of meats is deliciously satisfying for Sunday dinner, with enough leftovers to enjoy again during the week or to freeze for a treat at any time.

OIL AND LEMON SAUCE
Salmurigliu

Makes 1 cup, enough for 2 pounds fish or 2 pounds vegetables

¾ cup extra-virgin olive oil

¼ cup freshly squeezed lemon juice

Salt and black pepper to taste

1 clove garlic, crushed

1 twig dried oregano

Place all the ingredients in a bottle, then shake and splash on grilled fish or even grilled vegetables.

UNCOOKED TOMATO SAUCE
Sarsa crura

Makes enough sauce for 1 pound of spaghetti or macaroni

Serves 4 to 6

4 medium tomatoes

2 cloves garlic, chopped

2 tablespoons chopped fresh basil leaves

Salt and red pepper flakes to taste

¼ cup extra-virgin olive oil

Bring a small pot of water to the boil and dip each of the tomatoes in the boiling water for 30 seconds. Drop into cold water, and take the peel off. Chop the tomatoes. Add the garlic, basil, salt, pepper, and olive oil. Mix and let stand while you cook the pasta.

PARSLEY SAUCE

Sarsa ri putrisinu

Makes 1 cup, enough for 2 pounds of meat or fish

Serves 4 to 6

½ bunch Italian flat-leaf parsley

2 cloves garlic

2 strips lemon peel

2 tablespoons salted capers, rinsed or capers in vinegar, drained

½ cup extra-virgin olive oil

Juice of 2 lemons

Salt and pepper to taste

Chop the parsley, garlic, and the lemon peel finely by hand. Coarsely chop the capers, and add to the parsley with the olive oil, lemon juice, salt, and pepper. Mix well, and let stand until ready to serve. This sauce is excellent on fish or on boiled meats or even on potatoes.

WHITE RICOTTA SAUCE

Ricotta arruminata

Makes enough for 1 pound of pasta

Serves 4 to 6

2 cups fresh ricotta cheese

¼ to ½ cup pasta cooking water or milk

Salt and pepper to taste

¼ cup extra-virgin olive oil

Place the ricotta in a bowl. Thin it with either the pasta cooking liquid or with milk, and add salt, pepper, and oil. Add to any drained cooked pasta, stir, and serve with grated Italian pecorino, caciocavallo, or Parmigiano cheese.

OIL AND GARLIC SAUCE
Sarsa ri agghiu e uogghiu

Makes enough for 1 pound of pasta

Serves 4 to 6

⅓ to ½ cup extra-virgin olive oil

4 cloves garlic, chopped

Red pepper flakes to taste

½ cup pasta or vegetable
cooking water

Heat the olive oil, add the garlic and red pepper flakes so that both ingredients release their fragrance. Just as the garlic begins to color, add the pasta or vegetable cooking liquid to keep the garlic from burning. This sauce will season 1 pound of pasta, or 2 heads of blanched escarole, or 1 pound of fresh spinach.

ANCHOVY SAUCE
Sarsa ri anciuovi

Makes enough for 1 pound of pasta

Serves 4 to 6

⅓ to ½ cup extra-virgin olive oil

4 cloves garlic, chopped

Red pepper flakes to taste

1 (4-ounce) can flat anchovy
fillets

½ cup pasta or vegetable
cooking water

Heat the olive oil, add the garlic and the red pepper flakes, and cook for 1 minute. Add the anchovies, and let them melt into the oil. If using for pasta or vegetables add the cooking liquid before mixing in the drained pasta or the vegetables. This sauce is excellent for pasta, escarole, cauliflower, or broccoli.

TUNA SAUCE

Sarsa ri tunnu

Makes enough sauce for 1 pound of spaghetti

Serves 4 to 6

2 cloves garlic, chopped

¼ cup extra-virgin olive oil

1 (6-ounce) can tuna, packed in olive oil

1 (6-ounce) can tomato paste

Salt and pepper to taste

Sauté the garlic in the olive oil, and as it barely begins to color, add the tuna with its packing oil, and stir. Add the tomato paste, 2 tomato cans of water, salt, pepper, and stir again. Lower the heat, and simmer for 15 minutes.

TOMATO SAUCE

Sarsa ri pummaroru

Makes enough sauce for 1 pound of pasta

Serves 4 to 6

This is a delicious chunky sauce that is good with eggs, on pizza or on pasta.

¼ cup extra-virgin olive oil

2 cloves garlic, chopped

1 (28-ounce) can Italian peeled tomatoes

1 tablespoon sugar

Salt and pepper to taste

8 fresh basil leaves, chopped

Heat the olive oil, add the garlic, and as it begins to color, add the tomatoes, ½ can of water, the sugar, salt, pepper, and the basil. Lower the heat, and simmer for 30 minutes. As the sauce cooks, crush the tomatoes with a fork to break them down.

MAMA' MILINA'S SPICY TOMATO SAUCE

Sarsa piccanti ri mama' Milina

Makes about 4 cups, enough for 2 pounds of pasta

This sauce is delicious on pasta or pizza.

1 onion, chopped

¼ cup extra-virgin olive oil

1 (28-ounce) can Italian peeled tomatoes

1 tablespoon sugar

2 tablespoons salted capers, rinsed off

¼ teaspoon ground nutmeg

¼ teaspoon ground cloves

¼ teaspoon ground allspice

¼ teaspoon fennel seeds

Salt and red pepper flakes to taste

Sauté the onion in the olive oil. Add the tomatoes, sugar, capers, spices, salt, pepper, and ½ can of water. Stir, lower the heat, and cover. As the sauce cooks, stir it a few times, and crush the tomatoes with a fork or with a potato masher. Cook for 30 minutes.

MEAT SAUCE

*Use a small amount of this sauce for **Arancini** (page 20).
The rest can be frozen.*

½ pound <u>each</u> ground beef and ground pork, or all beef or all pork

½ cup grated cheese

1 egg

2 garlic cloves, finely chopped

2 tablespoons chopped Italian flat-leaf parsley

Salt and black pepper to taste

2 tablespoons extra-virgin olive oil

¾ cup red or white wine

2 (28-ounce) cans pureed tomatoes

1 tablespoon sugar

½ teaspoon crushed fennel seeds

1 pinch ground nutmeg

1 pinch ground allspice

1 pinch ground cloves

Mix the meat, cheese, egg, garlic, parsley, salt, and pepper. Heat the olive oil in a pan, add the meat mixture, and stir to crumble and brown evenly. Add the wine, stir, and cook for 5 minutes. Add the tomato puree, and 1 can of water. Season with the sugar, fennel, and spices to taste. Bring to the boil, then lower the heat to a slow simmer, cover, and cook for 1 hour.

SAUCE WITH MEATBALLS AND SAUSAGE

Ragu' cu purpitti e sausizza

Makes 10 cups

Sauce:

1 onion, chopped

1 carrot, chopped

1 stalk celery, chopped

2 tablespoons butter

2 tablespoons extra-virgin olive oil

2 (28-ounce) cans pureed tomatoes

1 tablespoon sugar

¼ teaspoon ground nutmeg

¼ teaspoon ground allspice

Pinch of ground cloves

Pinch of ground cardamom

Salt and pepper to taste

Meatballs and sausage:

½ pound each beef, pork, and veal, chopped

1 cup dried bread crumbs

½ cup grated cheese

2 eggs

¼ cup chopped Italian flat-leaf parsley

2 cloves garlic, chopped

Salt and pepper to taste

¼ cup extra-virgin olive oil

1 pound sweet or hot Italian sausage

1 cup wine

To prepare the sauce:

Sauté the onion, carrot, and celery in the butter and oil. Add the tomato puree and 1 can of water. Bring to the boil, add the sugar and spices, lower the heat, and cook, covered, for 1½ hours.

Meanwhile, prepare the meatballs:

Mix the chopped meats, bread crumbs, grated cheese, eggs, parsley, garlic, salt, and pepper well with your hands. Shape into small balls the size of a cherry, if you are making *Timballu ri pasta* (page 72) and fry them until brown in the oil. Make the meatballs larger, to serve with spaghetti or macaroni. As the meatballs are browned, drop them into the simmering tomato sauce.

To prepare the sausage:

Using kitchen shears, cut the sausage into 1-inch pieces, and brown in the same pan, adding them also to the sauce as they are cooked. Deglaze the frying pan with the wine, and add to the sauce.

SUNDAY MEAT SAUCE

Ragu' ra ruminica

Makes 4 quarts of sauce and meats, about 30 servings

This recipe makes enough for 20 people, including some second helpings. I make this when my husband and I volunteer to cook at the homeless shelter in Englewood, New Jersey, or at our own overflow shelter at Central Unitarian Church in Paramus, New Jersey. The guests are always delighted with the richness of flavor that this sauce adds to cooked spaghetti, and with the delicious variety of meats that complete the dinner. We always get compliments. Of course, if you are not cooking for 20 people, you can freeze the leftover sauce and meat. Because of the variety of meats in this sauce, it's not possible to make a small amount, but since it freezes very well, the leftovers make very quick meals anytime you feel like serving them.

1 onion, finely chopped

1 carrot, finely chopped

1 stalk celery finely chopped

2 tablespoons extra-virgin olive oil

3 (28-ounce) cans tomato puree

1 tablespoon sugar

½ teaspoon crushed fennel seeds

¼ teaspoon ground nutmeg

¼ teaspoon ground cloves

¼ teaspoon ground allspice

Pinch of ground cardamom

Salt and pepper to taste

2 Stuffed Pork Skins (page 85)

1 recipe Country-Style Spareribs, Sausages, Meatballs, and Chicken Legs (page 86)

Sauté the onion, carrot, and celery in the olive oil. Add the tomato puree and 1½ cans of water. Bring to the boil, add the sugar, fennel seeds, spices, salt, and pepper. Lower the heat, cover, and simmer, adding meats as they are ready. After all meats have been added, cover, and simmer for 1½ hours.

After the *ragu'* has cooled, take out the stuffed pork skins, remove the twine, and freeze separately with some of the sauce. When ready to serve, thaw, slice, and heat. Pack some of each of the remaining meats in 16-ounce freezer containers, filling them half-way, then covering the meats with sauce. When ready to use, thaw, heat the meats and the sauce, and thin it out with ½ cup of the spaghetti cooking water. Each container will be enough for 1 pound of spaghetti.

After the first meal for 6 to 8, the leftovers will yield about 6 pints.

STUFFED PORK SKINS
Cutini ri maiali cini

1 cup Toasted Bread Crumbs (page 68)

½ cup grated caciocavallo, Romano, or Parmigiano cheese

2 cloves garlic, chopped

2 tablespoons chopped Italian flat-leaf parsley

Salt and pepper to taste

1 egg, beaten

2 pork skins

2 hard-boiled eggs

Mix the bread crumbs, cheese, garlic, parsley, salt, and pepper. Bind the mixture by adding the beaten egg. Place the pork skins on the counter. Distribute the filling between them. Cut the hard-boiled eggs into quarters and place them on top of the filling. Roll the filled skins very carefully as you would a jelly roll, tie with kitchen twine, and add them to the simmering sauce.

When ready to serve, carefully remove the twine, and cut them into ½-inch slices. This is best done after they are cool. To reheat them, place on a platter in a single layer, cover them with plastic film, and microwave until hot.

COUNTRY-STYLE SPARE RIBS, SAUSAGE, MEATBALLS, AND CHICKEN LEGS

Cuostuli, sausizza, purpitti e cosci ri iaddina

¼ cup extra-virgin olive oil

1½ pounds country-style spare ribs

1½ pounds Italian hot or sweet sausage

1 recipe Meatballs (page 83)

6 chicken legs

1 cup white or red wine

Heat the oil in a large frying pan and brown the ribs in a single layer, without crowding them, until they are golden brown all over. As they brown drop them into the simmering sauce (page 84). Fry the sausage next; brown each piece all over, and drop them into the sauce. Brown the meatballs, drop them into the sauce. Finally brown the chicken legs and add to the sauce. When you have finished browning all the meats, deglaze the pan with the wine, scraping up all the brown bits, and add it to the sauce.

MEAT

Carni

Ragusa Ibla – Palazzo La Rocca

Although meat was traditionally eaten sparingly and mostly on Sundays and holidays as recently as 50 years ago, some wonderful dishes make a feast out of humble ingredients such as chicken legs. I buy the whole chicken, usually two at a time. I bone them, use whatever I need at the time, and freeze the rest for future use. My husband prefers white chicken meat, whereas I like dark meat. Howard jokes that this is one of the reasons that our marriage of 39 years has been so long-lasting!

Some time ago, on a trip to Ragusa, he decided to go shopping for chicken breasts. This was before frozen specialty cuts of meat were readily available. The butcher, who only had three fresh chickens on hand, brought the chickens out and cut out the breasts for my husband. He probably thought it a very strange request, since people bone their own chicken, and make use of everything including the bones for soup.

Pork sausage with fennel seeds is particularly flavorful in Sicily, and it's readily available in the United States, so delicious versions can be made in the American kitchen. Stuffed meat rolls are not only very tasty in themselves, but the cooking process produces a marvelous sauce to serve on pasta.

Lamb dishes from our Greek roots are quite different from anything you would have in Greece, and are certainly worth trying. The lamb pie is a real treat.

The most unusual dish is the meats in gelatin or *liatina*, which is a specialty of our cuisine, also well worth the time and effort to prepare. This is cooking for compliments!

SAUSAGE IN WINE

Sausizza co' vinu

Serves 6 to 8

The sausage will be easier to handle if it is in one piece,
but links are also fine.

2 pounds Italian sausage, preferably in one piece

1 cup red wine

Place the sausage in a frying pan that will hold it in a single layer. Cover the sausage with water, and cook until the water evaporates, about 30 minutes. Add the wine, and cook until the sausage is nicely browned, turning it once so that it browns evenly on all sides. Serve the sausage with the pan drippings, and good bread for dipping in the juices.

BAKED SAUSAGE, PEPPERS, AND POTATOES

Sausizza, pipi e patati 'nfurnati

Serves 6 to 8

I like red bell peppers for color, but green ones are fine.

2 pounds Italian hot or sweet sausage, or a combination of both

6 baking potatoes, cut in wedges

2 red bell peppers, cut into strips

¼ cup extra-virgin olive oil

Sprinkle of dried oregano ·

Salt and pepper to taste

Preheat the oven to 375 degrees. Separate the sausage links. Place the sausages, potatoes, and peppers in a large baking pan. Add the olive oil, oregano, salt, and pepper, and mix well. Bake for 1 hour, stirring the contents of the pan twice during baking to be sure that nothing sticks to the pan. Serve with a good crusty bread.

FELICE'S LEMON CHICKEN

Iaddina ca' lumia ri Fulici

Serves 6 to 8

My father Felice Bellia would barbecue this over charcoal in the summer, and bake it in the oven in the winter. The winter version has a sauce, but the summer variety is just as delicious.

2 chickens

¼ cup coarse salt

½ cup extra-virgin olive oil

¼ cup lemon juice

1 teaspoon dried oregano

Salt and pepper to taste

4 cloves garlic

1 lemon, thinly sliced

Soak the chickens in water to cover and the coarse salt for 30 minutes. Rinse them well, cut them into serving pieces, dry them with paper towels, and set aside.

Meanwhile, place the olive oil, lemon juice, oregano, salt, and pepper in a jar with a tight-fitting lid. Crush the garlic cloves, remove the skin, and add to the marinade in the jar, and shake vigorously to blend.

Place a layer of the chicken pieces in a glass bowl, spoon the marinade on top, and continue until all the chicken is used up. Pour leftover marinade on top, cover with plastic wrap, and refrigerate for several hours or overnight.

When ready to cook, preheat oven to 375 degrees. Remove the chicken pieces from the marinade, place on a rack in a roasting pan, and bake for 1¼ hours or until browned. Brush the chicken with marinade as it bakes, and add the remaining marinade to the pan juices after the chicken is done.

Place the roasting pan on top of the stove over 2 burners. Turn on the burners on medium heat. Add the lemon slices, and simmer for 3 minutes. Add 1 cup water to deglaze the pan, stir, bring back to the boil, and turn off the heat.

Place the chicken on a platter in a single layer, top with the lemon slices, being careful not to break them, and spoon the sauce over the chicken. Delicious both hot or at room temperature.

STUFFED CHICKEN LEGS

Cosci ri iaddina cini

Serves 8 to 12

1½ cups Toasted Bread Crumbs (page 68)

½ cup grated caciocavallo or pecorino Romano cheese

2 cloves garlic, chopped

2 tablespoons Italian flat-leaf parsley, chopped

Salt and pepper to taste

1 egg, beaten

¼ cup raisins

¼ cup pignoli (pine nuts)

6 chicken legs, boned

¼ cup extra-virgin olive oil

1 cup marsala wine

Mix the bread crumbs, cheese, garlic, parsley, salt, and pepper. Add the beaten egg together with the raisins and the pignoli. The mixture will be moist and crumbly. Place the boned chicken legs on the counter, skin side down. Divide the stuffing among the legs, close the skin around the stuffing, and tie with cotton string.

Heat the oil in a pan with a cover that will hold the stuffed chicken legs in a single layer. Place the legs in the hot oil, and brown all around. Add the marsala, and be sure that none of the pieces are stuck to the pan. Lower the heat, cover, and cook for 45 to 60 minutes or until tender. Check it from time to time and add a little water if it seems to be drying out. Let the chicken cool in its own juices.

When ready to serve, cut and remove the string, slice each leg into 3 pieces, place the pieces, cut side up, on a serving platter, and serve with the pan juices drizzled on top.

STEWED RABBIT OR CHICKEN

Cunigghiu o iaddina a ghiotta

Serves 4 to 6

¼ cup extra-virgin olive oil

1 rabbit or 1 chicken, cut into serving pieces

¼ cup white wine vinegar

1 onion, chopped

2 stalks celery, cut in ½-inch slices

2 tablespoons capers, packed in salt or vinegar, rinsed

2 tablespoons pitted and sliced green olives

Salt and pepper to taste

1 cup white wine

Heat the olive oil in a large frying pan that will hold the meat in a single layer. Brown the meat on all sides, add the vinegar, and turn the meat so that all the pieces are flavored as the vinegar evaporates. Add the onion, celery, capers, olives, salt, pepper, and wine. Reduce the heat to a simmer, cover the pan, and continue to cook for 45 to 50 minutes or until done. Check once in a while to be sure that it doesn't dry out. If necessary, add water ¼ cup at a time. Serve hot or at room temperature; this is delicious either way.

STUFFED BEEF ROLL
Farsumagru

2 pounds thin, flat beef cut for brasciole

2 slices mortadella or ham

1 cup Toasted Bread Crumbs (page 68)

½ cup grated caciocavallo or Romano cheese

2 cloves garlic, chopped

¼ cup chopped Italian flat-leaf parsley

Salt and pepper to taste

¼ cup pignoli (pine nuts)

1 egg, beaten

2 hard-boiled eggs, cut in half lengthwise

¼ cup extra-virgin olive oil

1 cup red wine

¼ cup tomato paste

2 bay leaves

Place the beef on the counter, cover with the mortadella slices. Meanwhile, mix the bread crumbs, cheese, garlic, parsley, salt, pepper and pignoli. Moisten with the beaten egg, and spread on top of the mortadella. Place the hard-boiled eggs in the middle of the piece of meat end to end, cut side down. Roll the meat away from you beginning on the long side, around the eggs and all the way to the other side. Tie the roll with kitchen twine so that the filling is enclosed and held in place.

Heat the oil in a pan large enough to hold the roll (I use a fish poacher) and brown the meat all around. Add the wine, and turn the roll so that the wine flavors every side. Add the tomato paste, and enough water to reach about $2/3$ of the way up the beef roll. Bring to the boil, reduce the heat, add the bay leaves, cover, and simmer for $1^{1}/4$ to $1^{1}/2$ hours, or until tender when pierced with a knife. Remove from the heat, and let rest for 30 minutes. Remove the twine, slice, and serve with the pan juices.

ROAST LEG OF LAMB

Coscia ri agnieddu arrustuta

Serves 6 to 8

My brother Carmelo Bellia sometimes cooks this leg of lamb for Christmas dinner by hanging it with a string on a hook in the front of the fireplace, so that whoever comes near it gives the string a twist, allowing the meat to turn and to cook evenly.

½ head garlic

½ bunch Italian flat-leaf parsley

8 ounces caciocavallo or provolone cheese

1 leg of lamb

Salt and pepper to taste

2 (10-ounce) packages frozen baby lima beans

Preheat the oven to 350 degrees. Peel the garlic and cut each clove in quarters lengthwise. Separate the parsley sprigs, and cut the cheese into ¼-inch matchsticks. Using a small sharp knife, make incisions all over the leg of lamb. Fill each hole by pushing a piece of garlic, a sprig of parsley, and a slice of cheese with your index finger. When done, rub the meat with salt and pepper.

Place on a rack and roast for 30 minutes. Remove any fat which may have accumulated in the pan, add the lima beans, and continue to roast for 1 hour. Let rest for 20 minutes before carving.

EASTER LAMB PIE FROM RAGUSA

'Mpanata r'agnieddu Rausana

Serves 6 to 8

This is a very special Easter dish from Ragusa, my native city. Don't be put off by a meat pie that has bones. Instead, think of it as a lamb stew, which would normally have bones, except that in the 'mpanata, the meat is encased in bread dough. Because it cooks slowly and cools encased in crust, it is the most delicious lamb you've ever tasted. The 'mpanata can be made with boned and cubed leg of lamb, but it will not be as succulent. The filling needs to sit overnight, so start it a day early.

Filling

2 pounds lamb shoulder or leg, cubed with bones

2 cloves garlic, chopped

½ bunch Italian flat-leaf parsley, chopped

Salt and black pepper to taste

Dough

4 cups unbleached flour

1 tablespoon instant yeast (see page 7)

¼ cup lard or shortening

1 teaspoon salt

1 egg, beaten

Place the meat in a bowl, add the garlic, parsley, salt, and pepper, and mix well. Cover with plastic film, and refrigerate overnight.

Mix the flour and the yeast. Cut the lard into the flour, add 1¼ cups water and the salt, and mix the dough. This can be done in a mixer equipped with a dough hook, or in a food processor. Place the mixed dough on a floured surface, and knead until smooth and elastic, about 5 minutes. Place in a large bowl, spray with olive oil, turn, and spray the other side. Cover with plastic film, and let rise for 1½ hours or until doubled in bulk.

When ready to make the *'mpanata*, preheat the oven to 375 degrees. Divide the dough into a slightly larger and a smaller piece. Take the larger portion and roll it out into a circle to fit a 10 to 12-inch oiled pie plate. Fill the dough-lined pie plate with the lamb mixture. Roll out the smaller portion of dough into a circle to fit the top of the pie. Moisten the edges with water and seal top and bottom crust very well. Brush the top of the pie with the beaten egg, prick with a fork, and bake for 2 hours. After 1 hour in the oven, cover the pie with a piece of aluminum foil to keep the crust from browning too much.

Remove from the oven, cover with a clean dish towel, and then with a folded bath towel. Let the pie cool <u>very slowly</u> for 2 hours. Serve in wedges and caution your guests about the bones. After the pie has rested, the bottom crust will have absorbed all the meat juices, and it's a special treat.

TRIPE WITH PEAS

Trippa ca' prisella

**Serves 6 to 8 hearty eaters and many more
if your guests just want to be adventurous and taste it**

*My cousin Sadie Battaglia Occhipinti, who was a wonderful cook,
added a can of chickpeas to her tripe, and it was equally delicious.*

2 pounds honeycomb tripe

¼ cup extra-virgin olive oil

1 medium onion, chopped

2 cups tomato puree

½ teaspoon dried oregano

Salt and red pepper flakes to taste

1 (10-ounce) package frozen tiny tender peas

Wash the tripe, and drop into a pot of boiling water for 45 minutes. Drain, cool, and cut into pieces each about 2 inches wide. Cut each piece into ½-inch strips, and set aside.

Heat the olive oil, add the onion and cook until translucent but not browned. Add the tomato puree together with the oregano, salt, and pepper. Bring the sauce to the boil, add the tripe, lower the heat, cover, and simmer for 45 minutes. Add the frozen peas, cook for 2 minutes, turn off the heat, and let stand for 15 minutes or until serving time.

MEATS IN ASPIC

This is a wonderful dish that is a very special winter treat for my friends and family from Ragusa, but I have served it to American friends who have also come to appreciate it. Traditionally, this was made with only pork using most of the head and the feet to make the gelatin base. I add the chicken breast because my husband likes it, and mixing the meats makes the dish tastier and more visually appealing when you serve it. It's easy to make, but it takes a long time. The results are great!

2 pork hocks

4 pork ears (optional)

2 pounds boneless pork roast

2 pork or lamb tongues

2 whole chicken breasts

4 cups white vinegar

1 tablespoon whole black peppercorns

2 bay leaves

2 lemons, sliced

2 tablespoons salt

Wash all the meats. Bring the vinegar and 12 cups water to the boil. Add the pork hocks, feet, and ears if you chose to add them. Bring the pot back to the boil over high heat. Lower the heat to a simmer. Skim the surface of any foam that may accumulate, add the black peppercorns, bay leaves, lemon slices, and salt. Cover the pot, and simmer for 2 hours.

Add the pork roast and the tongues, and simmer for 1 hour. Add the chicken breasts and simmer for another 30 minutes. Strain the meats over a large bowl to collect the broth. Cool the broth and refrigerate overnight.

Cool the meat, remove all the bones, and set aside. Line a loaf pan with a double thickness of cheesecloth, and let the cheesecloth drape down the sides of the pan. Place the meat from the feet and the hocks, skin side down, in the bottom and up the sides of the pan. Fill the middle with the pork roast, chicken, and tongues. Use any remaining meat, skin side up, as a cover. You may have enough to fill 2 pans. Fold the cheesecloth over the top, and place a weight on the meats to pack them down. Refrigerate overnight.

The next day, take the broth out of the refrigerator, remove the layer of surface fat, and you will have a bowl of gelatin. Spoon the gelatin into a pot, and heat it just enough to dissolve it. Set it aside while you prepare the meats.

Continued

Unmold the meats, cut into ½-inch slices, place the slices on a platter in a single layer, and cover the meat slices with the warm gelatin. Cover with plastic wrap, and refrigerate again until the gelatin is set.

Serve a slice of the meats together with some of the gelatin. I serve this in a large ceramic quiche dish, because the sides of the pan allow you to cover the meats with gelatin.

You can also skip the molding procedure, and serve the *liatina* as my mother did, which was to put pieces of meat in deep dishes, and cover them with the gelatin. It keeps in the refrigerator ready to serve for 1 week.

FISH

Pisci

Modica

Fish is king in Sicily. Surrounded by the Mediterranean, there is a great variety of fish, which is caught, cooked, and eaten while the eyes are still bright. Tuna is still caught near Trapani, where it has been fished since time immemorial and where it's still fished by ancient methods in a tradition called the *mattanza*. Fresh tuna is delicious and unusual for Americans who, like my husband, had never had anything other than the canned variety.

Swordfish, which is thought to be best grilled and doused with *salmoriglio*, a fragrant sauce made of extra-virgin olive oil, lemon juice, oregano, garlic—just the basic ingredients—is as simple to make as it delicious. The most common way to prepare fish is to lightly flour it, fry it, and serve it with a squeeze of lemon.

FRIED SARDINES

Sardi fritti

Serves 4 to 6

1 cup flour

Salt and pepper to taste

2 pounds fresh sardines, cleaned

½ to 1 cup of canola or olive oil

1 lemon, quartered (optional)

Mix the flour, salt, and pepper. Roll the sardines in flour, shake off the excess, and set aside. Heat the oil in a large frying pan, add the sardines, and fry until crisp and delicately browned on both sides. Serve hot with lemon wedges if desired.

BAKED SARDINES WITH CHEESE

Sardi 'nfurnati co' caciu

Serves 4 to 6

This is a very unusual dish in that it includes cheese. Gourmets have been known to go to war over fish sauces served on spaghetti with grated cheese, but my father used to make this dish of baked sardines topped with cheese and it was delicious.

¼ cup extra-virgin olive oil

2 pounds fresh, sardines, cleaned

1½ cups Uncooked Tomato Sauce (page 77)

Salt and pepper to taste

Liberal sprinkle of dried oregano

4 ounces caciocavallo cheese, shaved

Preheat the oven to 375 degrees. Using 2 tablespoons oil, grease a baking pan that will hold all the sardines in a single layer. I use a large white ceramic quiche pan, and I arrange the fish in a circle. Spoon the tomato sauce over the sardines, sprinkle with salt, pepper, and oregano, and scatter the cheese shavings on top. Drizzle with the remaining 2 tablespoons olive oil, and bake for 35 to 40 minutes.

COD WITH GARLIC AND PARSLEY

Murruzzu sapuritu

Serves 4 to 6

Sometimes I take the leftover cooked cod, flake it, and use it together with the pan juices as a sauce for spaghetti. You can have it plain or topped with Toasted Bread Crumbs (page 68).

¼ cup extra-virgin olive oil

2 cloves garlic

2 tablespoons Italian flat-leaf parsley, chopped

2 pounds cod fillets

Salt and black pepper to taste

Heat the olive oil, add the garlic and sauté until it barely begins to color. Add the parsley, stir, and add the fish together with 1 cup of water. Season to taste with salt and pepper. Cover the pan, lower the heat, and cook for 20 minutes or until the fish is opaque and it flakes easily. Serve hot or at room temperature with crusty bread to dip into the juices.

GRILLED SWORDFISH

Piscispata co' salmurigliu

Serves 4

4 swordfish steaks

Salt and pepper to taste

½ cup of Oil and Lemon Sauce (page 77)

Season the swordfish steaks with salt and pepper and grill until done. Pass around the sauce for each guest to season the fish to his/her taste. You can also broil the fish and serve with the same sauce.

TUNA WITH ONIONS
Tunnu ca' cipudda

Serves 4 to 6

*My aunt Herminia Giacone Bellia won my husband over the first time
she made fresh tuna for our dinner when we were engaged to be married.*

½ cup extra-virgin olive oil

2 pounds fresh tuna

2 large onions, sliced

Salt and pepper to taste

2 tablespoons red wine vinegar

Heat ¼ cup of the oil in a frying pan, add the tuna, cook on both sides, and set aside. Add the remaining ¼ cup oil to the pan, add the sliced onions, and sauté them until translucent. Return the cooked tuna to the pan, salt and pepper to taste, mix, add the vinegar, and stir again to mix the flavors. Turn the heat off, and allow to cool in the same pan. Serve at room temperature.

CALAMARI WITH TOMATO SAUCE
Calamari co' pummaroru

Serves 6 to 8

¼ cup extra-virgin olive oil

2 cloves garlic, chopped

1 (28-ounce) can tomato puree

Salt and red pepper flakes to taste

2 pounds fresh calamari, cleaned

Heat the oil in a frying pan. Add the garlic, and before it begins to brown, add the tomato puree, and salt and pepper to taste. Bring to the boil, add the calamari, lower the heat, and simmer for 20 to 30 minutes. Serve hot with crusty bread or over cooked linguine.

COUSCOUS WITH FISH STEW

Cuscus Trapanese

Serves 6 to 8

Couscous, a North African import, is one of the most traditional dishes of Sicilian cuisine. Traditionally it is steamed for 1 hour in a special pot that holds the water on the bottom and the grain on top. The steam that comes through the holes of the tight fitting top of the pot is kept from dispersing by sealing the two pots with a strip of dough that is removed at the end of the cooking time.

1 (16-ounce) box plain couscous

2 pounds firm non-oily fish such as tile, monk, sea bass, grouper, or eel

2 pounds shrimp, calamari, and/or lobster

½ cup extra-virgin olive oil

4 cloves garlic, chopped

¼ cup chopped Italian flat-leaf parsley

2 pounds fresh tomatoes, peeled and chopped or 1 (28-ounce) can peeled tomatoes

4 bay leaves

Salt and black pepper to taste

Prepare couscous according to package directions.

If you bought whole fish, remove the heads and the tails and set them aside. Cut the fish into large pieces, separate the tentacles of the calamari from the body, remove the heads, and cut the bodies into rings. Shell the shrimp, and add the shells to the fish heads. If you are using lobsters, leave them whole for the final presentation. Wash the heads, tails, and shrimp shells, wrap them in a double thickness of cheesecloth, tie them securely, and refrigerate until ready to use.

Heat the olive oil in a large pot, add the garlic and sauté until it barely begins to color. Add the parsley, stir, then add the tomatoes. Add the fish heads in their cheesecloth, bay leaves, salt, and pepper. Add enough cold water to cover, bring the pot back to the boil, cover, lower the heat to simmer, and cook for 45 minutes. Remove the cheesecloth package from the pot, and discard.

Bring the pot back to the boil, add the calamari, simmer for 10 minutes, then add the fish. Simmer for another 10 minutes, then add the shrimp, and lobster, and simmer for another 5 minutes. Turn the heat off, and remove the fish with a skimmer. Strain the broth.

Place the prepared couscous on a large platter and pour 2 cups of strained fish broth over it. Cover the platter with aluminum foil, place a bath towel over it, and let stand for 30 minutes while the grains swell and absorb the broth. Meanwhile, bone the fish, and have it ready to add to the platter. When ready to serve, surround the couscous with pieces of fish, and top it with lobsters if you have used them.

DRIED COD STEW

Spizzatinu ri baccala'

Serves 4 to 6

2 pounds dried cod

Flour

2 pounds potatoes

¼ cup extra-virgin olive oil

1 onion, chopped

1 (28-ounce) can peeled plum tomatoes

Salt and black pepper to taste

When you buy the dried cod, ask how long it needs to be soaked. Some needs to be soaked for only one hour, while other types need to be soaked overnight, or even longer. Place the dried cod in a glass bowl, place the bowl in your kitchen sink, fill it with cold water, and soak the cod as long as necessary, changing the water a few times during the soaking period.

Cut the soaked fish into chunks, lightly flour the pieces of fish, and set aside. Peel, wash, and dry the potatoes, then quarter them, and set aside.

Heat the olive oil in a wide sauté pan with a cover. Fry the fish until delicately browned on both sides. Add the onion to the pan, and stir until it becomes limp. Lightly crush the peeled tomatoes, and add them to the pan together with salt and pepper to taste. Bring the pot to the boil, add the potatoes, turn the heat down, cover, and simmer for 1 hour.

Stir twice during the cooking period and add water ¼ cup at a time if the sauce gets too thick. Serve with crusty bread to soak up the delicious sauce.

SIDE DISHES
Cuntuorni

Caltagirone – Bandstand in the gardens

If fish is the king of food, then vegetables are the queens of Sicilian cuisine. I though it odd when I first came to the United States that children were told that if they didn't eat their spinach, they would not get any dessert. I had never heard of a child having to be coaxed into eating spinach! To everybody I knew, vegetables were as delicious as any dessert.

We always thought that my mother, who missed Ragusa more that any other member of the family, exaggerated when she described the Sicilian vegetables as being so much tastier than their American equivalents. We thought that she was romanticizing because she missed her birthplace, but when we began to return to Sicily as adults, we discovered that she was right, flavors are more powerful, fragrances are more pungent, and colors are more intense.

The freshness of all foods, and vegetables in particular, is of paramount importance. People still take pleasure in going to the country to pick wild greens which are always more flavorful than their cultivated varieties. Even in the United States, my husband and I go picking dandelions wherever we can find them, earning us the gratitude of friends who know them only as weeds in their manicured lawns. They are nature's own tonic, a harbinger of spring, and delicious to eat. Picking *cicoria* gives you exercise, and a free meal. Sicilians will eat any green, root, or vegetable that will go through the digestive system, and make it palatable, too. The best condiment for even a boiled green or vegetable is a drizzle of delicious cold-pressed olive oil and a sprinkle of salt.

ASPARAGUS

2 pounds asparagus

2 cloves garlic, chopped

¼ cup extra-virgin olive oil

10 sprigs Italian flat-leaf parsley, chopped

Salt and pepper to taste

Wash the asparagus, snap off the tough ends, and reserve for soup (page 49). Sauté the garlic in the olive oil, and before it browns, add the parsley and stir to mix and to keep from burning. Add the asparagus together with ½ cup of water, cover, and cook for 5 to 7 minutes, occasionally shaking the pan so that they cook evenly. Add salt and black pepper to taste. Serve warm or at room temperature.

JERUSALEM ARTICHOKES

Jerusalem artichokes are the tubers of a type of sunflower. Jerusalem is a corruption of the Italian word girasole, which means sunflower, and they were called artichokes because like the better-known vegetable, they also leave a sweet aftertaste in the mouth.

2 pounds Jerusalem artichokes (sun chokes)

¼ cup extra-virgin olive oil

2 cloves garlic, chopped

2 tablespoons Italian flat-leaf parsley, chopped

Salt and pepper to taste

Jerusalem artichokes are difficult to peel, but since the skin is edible, they can be scrubbed clean with a brush, or if you wish to remove the papery skin, you can easily scrape it off with a paring knife. Clean the Jerusalem artichokes, and cut them in little chunks. Heat the oil in a saucepan, add the garlic, and before it begins to color, add the parsley. Stir the garlic and the parsley, add the Jerusalem artichokes, stir again, add salt and pepper and ½ cup of water. Lower the heat, cover, and cook for 10 to 15 minutes or until tender.

SAUTÉED BROCCOLI RAPE

Bruocculi rapi affucati

Yields about 4 cups

I always make more than I need, since leftovers are delicious as a cold side dish, or they can enrich a dish of spaghetti. One bunch is enough for an omelet, but if you make 2 or 3 bunches you can make Spaghetti with Broccoli Rape (page 66) for another day. For 2 to 3 bunches use ½ cup of extra-virgin olive oil.

2 bunches broccoli rape

½ cup extra-virgin olive oil

2 cloves garlic, chopped

Salt and red pepper flakes to taste

Break the florets and the tender leaves from the stems. Strip the tougher leaves from their stems and add to the florets. Reserve the stems to make a stock in which to cook pasta. Wash and drain.

Heat ¼ cup of the olive oil in a large pan that will hold all the washed broccoli rape; add the garlic and barely brown. Add the broccoli rape, salt, and red pepper flakes. Cover and cook for 7 to 10 minutes turning the broccoli rape several times to ensure even cooking. It will cook down.

Using tongs, remove the broccoli rape from the pan so that they don't cook any further. Place on a platter and season with the remaining ¼ cup of the olive oil. The best flavor of the olive oil comes out when it's used uncooked to season a dish.

Note: Add 6 cups of water to the pan juices, bring it to the boil, add the reserved stems of the broccoli rape, cover, and simmer for 45 minutes. Put everything through a food mill, and use this very flavorful broth to cook 1 pound of spaghetti.

FRESH SPRINGTIME DANDELIONS

Cicuoria frisca

Serves 6 to 8

Dandelions are a natural diuretic and a liver tonic. They are rich in vitamins, beta-carotene, ascorbic acid, and very high in lecithin, which is being studied as a preventative for cirrhosis. Pick the dandelions in areas that don't have too much traffic, as they tend to absorb exhaust pollutants where there is heavy traffic. Also avoid chemically treated lawns.

Pick the whole head and remove the outer leaves and the flowers when you clean them. A bagful will yield only a dish of greens because, like all leafy vegetables, they cook down dramatically. During World War II, my grandmother Concettina roasted the roots, ground them, and made a coffee surrogate.

1 bag (2 to 4 pounds) wild dandelions

¼ cup coarse salt

¼ cup extra-virgin olive oil

Salt and red pepper flakes to taste

1 lemon

Carefully cut the root off of each bunch of dandelions and discard. Remove any dried or yellowed outer leaves, as well as any flowers. Drop the greens in a large bowl of cold water to which you have added the salt. The salt helps to dislodge the earth around the roots and between the leaves. Indeed, the hardest part of the preparation is the cleaning and washing. After all have been cleaned and allowed to soak in the salt water, take them out of the bowl, throw the water out, refill the bowl with clean cold water, swish the dandelions in the water, and repeat this procedure until you see no sand or earth in the bottom of the bowl. Then do it once more to be absolutely sure that they are clean.

Bring 8 cups of water to the boil, add the greens, bring the water back to the boil, lower the heat to a simmer, and cook 15 to 20 minutes or until tender. Using tongs, lift the cooked dandelions from the water, place in a serving dish, and season with salt, pepper, and olive oil.

The cooking water is slightly bitter, and I love the taste. I drink it cold with a pinch of salt and a squeeze of fresh lemon, as one would drink an herbal tea. According to my grandmother Concettina, it's very good for you. She called it a spring tonic, but it's definitely an acquired taste.

ZUCCHINI WITH VINEGAR

Cucuzzeddi c'acitu

Serves 6 to 8

4 medium zucchini

½ cup extra-virgin olive oil

6 cloves garlic, thinly sliced

Salt and pepper to taste

¼ cup red wine vinegar

Peel or scrub the zucchini very well, cut into ½-inch rounds, and set aside. Heat the olive oil in a large frying pan, add the garlic and fry until crisp and golden. Remove the garlic from the frying pan, and set aside. Fry each zucchini round in the garlic-flavored olive oil until delicately browned on both sides. As you fry each layer, dust with salt and pepper. When all the zucchini are cooked, put them all back in the pan, and holding a cover over the pan, lift one side, pour in the vinegar, and close the cover. Shake the pan for a minute and turn off the heat. Spoon the zucchini onto a glass or ceramic platter, top with the fried garlic, and let cool in its own juices until it reaches room temperature.

BATTER-FRIED ZUCCHINI

Cucuzzeddi fritti

Serves 4 to 6

2 eggs

¼ cup flour

Salt and pepper to taste

2 zucchini, peeled and cut into eighths lengthwise

½ cup vegetable oil

Beat the eggs with the flour and ¼ cup water, salt, and pepper. Cut each piece of the zucchini in half, dip each piece in the batter and fry in hot vegetable oil. Drain the oil off on paper towels. Season with salt and pepper while zucchini are hot. Serve immediately.

FRIED ZUCCHINI FLOWERS

Sciuri ri cucuzzeddi fritti

Serves 4 to 6

Zucchini flowers are a great treat, and are very easy to grow. We plant zucchini in our garden just for the flowers, since they are not always available in grocery stores. You can substitute tiger lily flowers, which grow on the side of the road, and are not only edible but delicious. The buds can also be cooked like asparagus.

2 eggs

¼ cup flour

Salt and pepper to taste

12 zucchini flowers

½ cup vegetable oil

Beat the eggs with the flour, ¼ cup water, salt, and pepper. Dip each flower in the batter, and fry in the hot oil until very delicately browned on both sides. Drain on paper towels, dust with a little salt and serve hot.

BATTER-FRIED CAULIFLOWER

Sciuriddi fritti

Serves 6 to 8

1 head cauliflower

Batter for Fried Zucchini Flowers

1 cup vegetable oil

Blanch the cauliflower in boiling water for 10 minutes or until you can pierce the core with a knife. Remove from the pot, and drop into a bowl of cold water. Remove the core, and separate the florets. Dip each one in the batter, and fry until golden in the hot oil. Drain on paper towels, and serve hot.

PEAS WITH MINT

Prisella ca' menta

Serves 4 to 6

¼ cup extra-virgin olive oil

1 medium onion, chopped

1 (10-ounce) package frozen tender tiny peas

Salt and black pepper to taste

4 sprigs fresh mint, chopped

Heat the olive oil in a small pan. Add the onion and sauté until browned. Add the frozen peas and ¼ cup of water. Salt and pepper to taste, lower the heat, cover, and cook for 5 minutes. Add the mint just before you turn off the heat, mix, and let rest for 5 minutes before you serve them. They are delicious hot or at room temperature.

GRILLED EGGPLANT WITH MINT SAUCE

Mulinciana ca' sarsa ri menta

Serves 6 to 8

2 eggplants

½ cup mint, chopped

¼ cup Italian flat-leaf parsley, chopped

2 cloves garlic, chopped

½ cup extra-virgin olive oil

¼ cup lemon juice

Grated peel of 1 lemon

Salt and pepper to taste

Slice the eggplants with the skin on, grill on both sides and arrange on a platter, overlapping the slices. Place the mint, parsley, and garlic in a food processor. Add the olive oil, lemon juice, lemon peel, salt, and pepper, and pulse a few times to blend. Spoon the sauce over the eggplant, cover with plastic wrap and let marinate at least one hour or until ready to serve.

EGGPLANT LAYERED WITH CHEESE

Mulinciana 'ncaciata

Serves 12

My friend Josephine Schinina' Lissandrello shared this recipe with me after she married Vincent in the beautiful baroque Cathedral of San Giorgio in Ragusa Ibla. I use two hinged frying pans (Italian frittata pans) to make this dish. In the absence of a frittata pan, use a large frying pan. After the first side is browned, place a platter on top of the pan, and turn the eggplant onto the platter. Place the same pan on the stove, add a little more extra-virgin olive oil, slide the eggplant back into the frying pan, and brown the second side. It's worth buying a frittata pan on your next trip to Italy, and while you're at it, buy a small and a large one. They are very useful.

2 eggplants

Salt

1 cup canola oil

¼ cup extra-virgin olive oil

¾ cup dried bread crumbs

¾ cup tomato sauce

1½ cups grated caciocavallo or provolone cheese

Slice the eggplant, sprinkle with salt, and stack the slices putting a filled tea kettle on top as a weight; this will press the slices and squeeze out the bitter juices. Let them drain for 30 minutes. Rinse the slices, pat dry with paper towels, fry in canola oil, and set aside.

Drizzle a hinged frying pan with 2 tablespoons of the olive oil and lightly coat with half of the bread crumbs. Make a layer of eggplant, spread a spoonful (very little) of tomato sauce on the eggplant, and top with abundant grated cheese. Continue to layer eggplant, sauce, and cheese, ending with eggplant and a coating of the remainder of the bread crumbs. Drizzle the remaining 2 tablespoons of the olive oil on top of the bread crumbs. Place on the stove, and heat slowly while gently shaking the pan to be sure that nothing sticks. When you are confident that the first side is nicely browned, when you begin to smell the eggplant, turn the pan to brown the other side. Unmold onto a pedestal platter, and serve in wedges at room temperature.

ESCAROLE WITH OIL AND GARLIC

Scarola agghiu e uogghiu
Serves 6 to 8

1 head escarole

Salt to taste

½ cup extra-virgin olive oil

4 cloves garlic, sliced

Red pepper flakes to taste

Wash the escarole in several changes of water. Bring 2 quarts of water to the boil, add salt to taste, drop the washed escarole in the pot, and simmer for 10 minutes. Using tongs, lift the cooked escarole out of the water, and set aside. Reserve the cooking water for soup or cooking spaghetti.

Heat the olive oil in a large frying pan, fry the garlic until golden brown. Remove the garlic and set aside. Add the escarole to the oil in the pan, add salt and red pepper flakes to taste, and turn with tongs so that the escarole is flavored and heated through. Spoon onto a serving platter, top with the fried garlic, and serve immediately or after it cools to room temperature.

OVEN-BROWNED POTATOES

Patati 'nfurnati
Serves 6 to 8

¼ cup extra-virgin olive oil

2 pounds potatoes, cut into quarters

Salt and pepper to taste

Sprinkle of dried oregano

Preheat oven to 350 degrees. Coat a baking pan with olive oil or vegetable oil spray. Put the potatoes in the pan, drizzle with olive oil, sprinkle with salt, pepper, and oregano, and mix well. Bake for 1 hour. Stir the potatoes twice during the cooking time so that they brown evenly. Serve hot.

POTATO, PEPPER, AND ONION CASSEROLE
Patati, pipi e cipudda

Serves 6 to 8

6 potatoes

2 bell peppers, cut into strips

2 large onions, cut into thick slices

½ cup extra-virgin olive oil

Salt and black pepper to taste

Sprinkle of oregano

Preheat the oven to 350 degrees. Cut the potatoes into wedges and place in an oil-sprayed baking pan. Add the peppers and onions. Mix in the olive oil, salt, pepper, and oregano. Bake for one hour. Stir twice during the cooking time to be sure that everything browns evenly.

CARROTS WITH CAPERS
Vastunachi che' ciapparieddi

Serves 6 to 8

6 carrots

4 garlic cloves, sliced

¼ cup extra-virgin olive oil

2 tablespoons salted capers, rinsed

Salt and red pepper flakes to taste

2 tablespoons red wine vinegar

Peel, wash, and cut the carrots into matchsticks. Sauté the garlic in the olive oil, and add the carrots, capers, salt, and red pepper. Stir for about 1 minute. Add ½ cup of water, cover, and cook for 5 minutes. Take the cover off, stir-fry to evaporate all the water, and to complete cooking. Add the vinegar, immediately cover to prevent splashing, shake the pan to mix everything, and turn the heat off. Serve at room temperature or even chilled.

CHICKPEAS WITH FENNEL

Ciciri che' finuocci

Serves 4 to 6

The feathery leaves of the fennel bulbs, which are easily available in all supermarkets, are fine, although fresh dill is probably closer to the "wild fennel" available in Sicily.

2 fennel bulbs or 2 generous bunches fresh dill

1 cup dried chickpeas, soaked overnight, or 2 (16-ounce) cans cooked chickpeas

Salt and pepper to taste

¼ cup extra-virgin olive oil

Cut the leaves off the fennel and reserve the bulbs for salad. Discard the very tough leaves, wash, drain, and chop the leaves, and set aside until ready to cook. If using dried soaked chickpeas, drain, rinse, and drain again before placing them in a pot. Cover the chickpeas with 2 quarts of cold water. Place the pot on the stove, bring to the boil, then lower the heat to a simmer, cover the pot, and cook for 1½ hours or until tender.

If using canned chickpeas, simply bring 4 cups water to the boil, and add the chickpeas with their liquid to it.

Add the fennel leaves, and cook another 30 minutes. Using a skimmer, take most of the chickpeas and fennel from the broth, place them in a serving dish, season with salt, pepper, and olive oil. Serve either hot or at room temperature, with good bread. Reserve the broth for Chickpea Soup (page 55).

LENTILS WITH BROCCOLI

Linticcia cui bruocculi

Serves 6 to 8

Lentils must soak overnight, so plan ahead.

1 pound lentils

1 bunch fresh broccoli

½ cup extra-virgin olive oil

Salt and red pepper flakes to taste

1 lemon, cut into wedges (optional)

To cook perfect lentils: Pick over the lentils, rinse, place them in a pot, and add 6 cups of cold water. Bring the water and lentils to the boil, and simmer over low heat for 10 minutes. Turn the heat off, cover, and let stand overnight in the broth.

Trim and wash the broccoli. Cut the florets into serving pieces. Peel and chop the stems, strip the leaves from their stalks, and set aside for soup.

Using a skimmer, remove most of the lentils, from the pot, place them in a bowl, and set aside. Bring the broth back to the boil, add the broccoli florets, cook for 5 minutes or until crisp-tender. Remove the broccoli from the pot with tongs, place them in a bowl, and reserve the broth for Lentil Soup (page 56).

Divide the olive oil between the lentils and the broccoli. Toss each separately adding salt to the cooked broccoli and salt and red pepper flakes to the lentils. Spoon the lentils onto a platter and place the broccoli around the lentils. Place lemon wedges between the broccoli and the lentils, and serve at room temperature with crusty bread.

BEANS WITH CELERY

Casola cu l'acciu

Serves 4 to 6

Dry beans must be soaked, so plan accordingly.

½ bunch celery, including leaves

1 pound dried white cannellini or red kidney beans, soaked overnight, or 2 (16-ounce) cans white cannellini or red kidney beans, undrained

Salt and pepper to taste

¼ cup extra-virgin olive oil

Wash, drain, and chop the celery including the leaves. If using soaked beans, drain, rinse, and drain again before placing in a pot and covering with 2 quarts of cold water. Place the pot on the stove, bring to the boil, then lower the heat to a simmer, cover the pot, and cook for 1½ to 2 hours or until tender. Add the chopped celery and cook 30 minutes.

If using canned beans, bring 4 cups of water to the boil, add the celery, and cook for 20 minutes. Then add the canned beans with their juice and cook another 10 minutes

Using a skimmer, take most of the beans and celery from the broth, and reserve the rest for Bean Soup (page 57). Place the cooked beans and celery in a serving dish. Season with salt, pepper, and olive oil, and serve with good crusty bread either hot or at room temperature.

SALADS *'Nzalati*

Ragusa Ibla – Cattedrale di San Giorgio

Salads are usually served as a refreshing light course after the meal. Traditionally, salads, accompanied by good homemade bread together with some olives or a piece of cheese, were very often the meal.

The first time I made orange salad, and my husband saw that I dressed a fruit with salt, pepper, and olive oil, he wasn't sure that he even wanted to try it. But once he tasted it, he fell in love with it, and since then we have enjoyed it very often.

Salads are dressed with salt, pepper, extra-virgin olive oil, and either vinegar or lemon juice unless there are tomatoes or citrus fruits in the salad. The dressing is not premixed. Instead, salt and pepper are mixed in first, then the olive oil is drizzled on the salad and is mixed in, and finally the vinegar or lemon juice added. The proportions are 2 to 3 times more oil than vinegar or lemon juice. These proportions can be altered to one's own taste. I always dress the salad in a large bowl that allows me to mix it and to distribute the olive oil and the vinegar or lemon juice very well. Of course, I do this in the kitchen using the best tools for the job—my scrupulously clean hands—then transferring the salad to the serving dish, bowl, or platter.

If basil and mint are added to a salad, or to any dish, they are always added fresh. Oregano, on the other hand, is always added dried. Parsley, if used, is always Italian flat-leaf parsley; don't substitute the curly variety and never substitute cilantro, which is very similar in shape but very different in flavor. Basil, mint, and parsley, which are so basic to Sicilian cooking, can be grown very easily in a garden or even in pots.

ORANGE SALAD

'Nzalata ri aranci

Serves 4 to 6

4 oranges

Salt and red pepper flakes to taste

2 tablespoons extra-virgin olive oil or more to taste

Peel the oranges, cut them into a bowl in chunks, season them with salt and pepper, and drizzle with olive oil. Mix well before spooning into the serving bowl or platter. Use a little more olive oil if you would like to try the time-honored custom of dipping a good piece of bread in the salad juices.

ORANGE AND FENNEL SALAD

'Nzalata ri aranci e finuocciu

Serves 4 to 6

2 oranges

1 fennel bulb

Salt and pepper to taste

2 tablespoons extra-virgin olive oil or more to taste

1 tablespoon lemon juice

Peel the oranges, and cut them into a bowl in chunks. Remove the feathery leaves from the fennel bulb and reserve for soup (page 55), or to add to chickpeas (page 118). Cut the fennel bulb into quarters and slice thinly through the core so that the bulb remains attached. Sprinkle with salt and pepper and mix well. Drizzle with olive oil and mix again. Add the lemon juice and mix for the last time before transferring to a serving platter.

LEMON SALAD

'Nzalata ri lumia

Serves 6 to 8

This is served more as a relish than a salad, and a little goes a long way. You also need large lemons with thick skin, which are sometimes available in Italian markets.

1 large thick skinned lemon

¼ cup extra-virgin olive oil

½ teaspoon salt

Red pepper flakes to taste

Peel the lemon taking off only the yellow skin, but leaving the white pith. Cut the lemon in 4 lengthwise, and slice each quarter paper-thin. Place in a bowl, add the salt and mix well. Add the oil and the red pepper and mix again. Let stand for at least 15 minutes before serving. This salad is delicious eaten with bread dipped in the juices. The addition of the salt, and the bread tone down the acidity of the lemon.

ROMAINE AND CUCUMBER SALAD

'Nsalata ri lattuca e citriolu

Serves 6 to 8

1 head romaine lettuce

1 cucumber

6 sprigs fresh mint (optional)

Salt and pepper to taste

¼ cup extra-virgin olive oil

2 tablespoons red wine vinegar

Remove any of the tough outer lettuce leaves, and reserve them for soup. Wash the rest, spin dry, cut the leaves into ½-inch pieces, and place in a bowl. Peel the cucumber, quarter it lengthwise, cut into ½-inch pieces, and add to the romaine lettuce. Chop the mint leaves into very thin shreds and add to the salad. Sprinkle with salt and pepper, mix, drizzle with oil, and mix again. Add the vinegar and toss the salad. Transfer to a serving platter.

CUCUMBER AND PARSLEY SALAD

'Nzalata ri citriolu co' putrisinu

Serves 6 to 8

2 cucumbers

Salt and pepper to taste

1 clove garlic, chopped

6 sprigs Italian flat-leaf parsley, finely shredded

2 tablespoons extra-virgin olive oil

Juice of ½ lemon

Peel the cucumbers, quarter them lengthwise, and cut them into ½-inch slices. Place them in a bowl, add salt, pepper, garlic, parsley, olive oil, and lemon juice. Toss well and transfer to a serving dish.

ONION AND TOMATO SALAD

'Nsalata ri cipudda e pummaroru

Serves 4 to 6

I always peel tomatoes, but if you don't think it's necessary you don't have to peel them.

1 onion

4 tomatoes

Salt and pepper to taste

¼ cup extra-virgin olive oil

Few pinches of dried oregano

Slice the onion thinly, and soak in a bowl of cold water while you prepare the tomatoes. To peel the tomatoes, bring a small pot of water to the boil, immerse a tomato, count to 10, take it out of the boiling water, and plunge it into cold water. The skin will slip right off. Cut the tomatoes into wedges and place in a bowl. Take the onion out of the water, squeeze it dry between your hands, add it to the tomatoes, then add the salt, pepper, olive oil, and oregano. Toss well, and transfer to a serving platter.

POTATO AND ONION SALAD

'Nzalata ri patati e cipuddi

Serves 4 to 6

4 medium potatoes, unpeeled

2 medium onions, unskinned

Salt and black pepper to taste

2 cloves garlic, chopped

¼ cup extra-virgin olive oil

2 tablespoons red wine vinegar

Bring 2 quarts of water to the boil, add the unpeeled potatoes, and simmer for 10 minutes. Add the unskinned onions, and cook together for another 30 minutes. Strain and let cool.

Peel the potatoes, cut them into chunks, and place in a bowl. Skin the onions and quarter them. Add salt, pepper, garlic, olive oil, and vinegar, and toss delicately but well.

SCALLION AND CAPER SALAD

'Nzalata ri cipudduzzi e ciapparieddi

Serves 6 to 8

2 bunches scallions

2 tablespoons capers in salt, rinsed

¼ cup extra-virgin olive oil

2 tablespoons red wine vinegar

Clean the scallions and trim away the green leaves. Cut each scallion in quarters lengthwise. Place them in a glass container, add the capers, oil, and vinegar. Mix them well, and allow the salad to marinate for at least 1 hour. Serve in small quantities since it's quite pungent.

SAVORY PIES
Scacci e sfuogghiu

Concetta Sirugo Bellia, 1986

Sicilian *scaccie*, or what we may describe as savory pies, are as unique as they are delicious. The Easter Lamb Pie on page 95 is a specialty of Ragusa and worth every bit of effort to make. None of these wonderfully delicious dishes are found in restaurants, but all of them are made in the home both in Sicily and in the American homes of Sicilians.

They are ideal picnic foods since they are usually eaten warm or at room temperature. *Scaccie* are excellent party food since, cut into small pieces, they serve a lot of people. Since the crusts are made from bread dough, they are more substantial than a flaky pie crust. A wedge of *scaccia* can be eaten with the hands, not unlike a sandwich, making it a perfect finger food for casual entertaining.

Several of the recipes include ricotta, which when combined with vegetables not only flavors them, but makes them sweet, creamy, and rich. For my grandmothers, the vegetables were seasonal. Their appearance in the market was expected with great anticipation, and they were enjoyed often while available. Now that practically everything is available year-round we can indulge our cravings at will anytime we wish to spend a day in the kitchen.

SAVORY PIE DOUGH
Pasta pi' scacci

Makes enough dough for 2 scaccie

8 cups flour

1 tablespoon instant yeast
(see page 7)

½ cup lard or shortening

1 tablespoon salt

Place the flour in the bowl of a mixer equipped with a dough hook. Add the yeast, and cut in the shortening, and add the salt. Pour in 2 cups warm tap water, add the salt, mix for 4 minutes at low speed, then knead at medium speed for 6 more minutes. To mix by hand, place the flour and the yeast in a large bowl, cut in the shortening and add the salt. Make a well in the center, add the water, and mix the flour from the edge into the middle, slowly incorporating all of the flour into the water. Turn the dough on to a floured surface, and knead until smooth and elastic. Place the dough in an oiled or sprayed bowl. Turn upside down to coat both sides, cover, and let rise until doubled in bulk, about 1 hour.

FOLDED PARSLEY BREAD

Scaccia co' putrisinu

Serves 8 to 12 or more if cut into small pieces for a party or for an appetizer

½ recipe Savory Pie Dough
(page 129)

1 bunch Italian flat-leaf parsley

2 cloves garlic, chopped

2 tomatoes, chopped

1 cup thinly sliced or shredded
caciocavallo or provolone
cheese

½ cup extra-virgin olive oil

Salt and pepper to taste

1 egg, beaten

Prepare the dough and set aside.

Mix the parsley, garlic, tomatoes, cheese, oil, salt, and pepper and set aside.

Preheat the oven to 375 degrees. Roll out the dough on a large surface (preferably on a Formica table) that has been liberally sprinkled with flour. Roll the dough as thinly as possible. Spread half of the filling over the whole surface of the dough using your hands to be sure that you cover it evenly. Fold two opposite ends (top and bottom) towards the middle, and spread half of the remaining filling on the flaps of dough that you have folded. Now fold the other two opposite ends (left and right) towards the center, ending up with a rectangle.

Spread the remaining filling on the dough that you have just folded. Finally fold into thirds, (as if you were folding a letter) ending up with a long and narrow rectangle. Carefully lift the folded *scaccia* off the surface and into a greased baking sheet. Brush with the egg, and prick the whole surface of the *scaccia* with a fork. Bake for 1 hour and 15 minutes. Remove from the oven, cover with a cotton towel, and then with a doubled bath towel so that it cools very slowly. Serve warm or at room temperature. When you cut this, the inside will be a stack of very thin layers that are as beautiful to look at as they are delicious to eat. I like to cut it in half lengthwise, to reveal the layers, and then into squares that stay attached on one of the three sides.

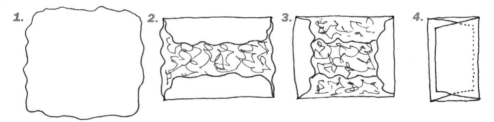

1. Roll out the dough on a well-floured surface

2. Spread half of the filling over the dough, and fold the top down and the bottom up

3. Continue folding always spreading more filling on the new folds of dough

FOLDED BASIL AND TOMATO BREAD
Scaccia co' basilico'

Serves 8 to 12 or more if cut into small pieces for a party or for an appetizer

½ recipe Savory Pie Dough (page 129)

2 cups fresh basil, chopped

2 cloves garlic, chopped

2 cups Tomato Sauce (page 80)

1 cup grated caciocavallo, pecorino, or provolone cheese

½ cup extra-virgin olive oil

Salt and pepper to taste

1 egg, beaten

Prepare the dough and set aside.

Mix the basil, garlic, Tomato Sauce, cheese, oil, salt, and pepper and set aside.

Proceed as directed in Folded Parsley Bread (page 130).

Variation
FOLDED BASIL AND TOMATO BREAD WITH CHEESE
Scaccia' co' basilico' e u caciu

Add 8 ounces of sliced caciocavallo, provolone, or Swiss cheese to the dough.

Variation
FOLDED BASIL AND TOMATO BREAD WITH EGGPLANT
Scaccia co' basilico' e a mulinciana

Add the fried slices of one eggplant to the dough. See page 115 for instructions on preparing and frying the eggplant.

SPINACH PIE

Scaccia ca' spinacia

Serves 6 to 8

½ recipe Savory Pie Dough (page 129)

2 (10-ounce) packages frozen spinach

1 onion, chopped

¼ cup extra-virgin olive oil

Salt and pepper to taste

½ cup raisins

½ cup coarsely chopped walnuts

1 egg, beaten

Prepare the dough and set aside. Thaw the spinach, squeeze between your hands to extract as much liquid as possible, and set aside. Sauté the onion in the olive oil, add the spinach, season with salt, and pepper and cook for 2 minutes. Add the raisins and the walnuts, mix, and turn off the heat.

Preheat oven to 375 degrees. Cut the dough into 2 pieces, making one piece slightly larger than the other. Take the larger piece, and roll out into a circle to fit a 12-inch pie plate. Spoon the filling into the dough-lined pan. Roll out the smaller piece of dough into a circle to fit the top of the pie plate. Cover the filling making sure that the top and bottom crust are well adhered by pressing around the circumference of the pie with the tines of a fork. Crimp the edge to be sure that it is closed.

Glaze the top with the beaten egg. Prick the surface in a decorative pattern. Bake for 1 hour and 15 minutes. Remove from the oven, and cover with a dishtowel and then a bath towel so that the *scaccia* cools gradually while the crust absorbs the juices. Let rest about 1 hour before serving. It will still be hot, although it's equally delicious at room temperature.

SPINACH AND JERUSALEM ARTICHOKE PIE

Scaccia ri spinaci e patacchi

Serves 6 to 8

½ recipe Savory Pie Dough (page 129)

2 (10-ounce) packages frozen spinach

1 pound Jerusalem artichokes

1 onion, chopped

¼ cup extra-virgin olive oil

Pinch of nutmeg

Salt and pepper to taste

Prepare the dough and set aside. Preheat the oven to 375 degrees.

Thaw the spinach, squeeze between your hands to extract as much liquid as possible, and set aside. Scrub the Jerusalem artichokes, cut into thick chunks, and set aside.

Sauté the onion in the olive oil, add the spinach, season with nutmeg, salt, and pepper and cook for 5 minutes. Add the Jerusalem artichokes and mix. Follow the directions for assembly of Spinach Pie on page 133.

LEEK AND RICOTTA PIE

Scaccia ri puorri e ricotta

Serves 6 to 8

½ recipe Savory Pie Dough (page 129)

2 leeks

¼ cup coarse kosher salt

1½ pounds ricotta

¼ cup extra-virgin olive oil

Black pepper to taste

Prepare the dough and set aside. Preheat the oven to 375 degrees.

Leeks require careful cleaning because they retain a lot of sand and earth. Cut them in half lengthwise, cutting away only the tough green leaves, but leaving the tender ones. Wash under running water until clean. Chop in ½-inch pieces, place in a bowl, stir the salt, and let stand for 30 minutes. Rinse the leeks, and taking them a handful at a time, squeeze out as much liquid as possible.

Place the leeks in a clean bowl, add the ricotta, olive oil, and pepper, and mix well. Follow the directions for assembly of Spinach Pie on page 133.

BROCCOLI AND SAUSAGE PIE

Scaccia ri bruocculi e sausizza

Serves 6 to 8

½ recipe Savory Pie Dough (page 129)

1 head broccoli

2 cloves garlic, chopped

½ cup Tomato Sauce (page 80)

¼ cup extra-virgin olive oil

Salt and pepper to taste

1 pound Italian pork sausage, casing removed

Prepare the dough and set aside. Preheat the oven to 375 degrees.

Wash the broccoli, spin dry, and cut the florets off the stems. Cut each floret head into 4 quarters through the core. Peel the stems, chop them, and add them to the tops. Season with the garlic, tomato sauce, olive oil, salt, and pepper. Follow the directions for assembly of Spinach Pie (page 133), placing the broccoli filling in first, then dotting the top with sausage meat. Continue Spinach Pie directions for top crust and baking.

SAUSAGE AND RICOTTA PIE

Sfuogghiu cu' ricotta e sausizza

Serves 6 to 8

My mother's way of rolling out the pastry for this pie made the top blossom with many layers that would open up during baking. You could substitute butter for the lard, but lard will make the crust very flaky and very flavorful. The variations use the very same ingredients, but shape it a little differently. All three are delicious.

½ recipe Savory Pie Dough (page 129)

¼ cup lard, melted and cooled

2 pounds ricotta

1 pound Italian pork sausage, casing removed

Preheat the oven to 375 degrees. Roll the dough into a thin rectangle (about 12 by 18 inches). Spread the lard on the whole surface, cut the dough into 1½-inch strips. Stack the strips one on top of the other, then carefully roll them from end to end into a flat cylinder. Cut the cylinder in half to make 2 circles. Roll out one circle and place in a 10 to 12-inch pie plate. Spoon the ricotta on top of the pastry-lined pie plate, and place the sausage on top of the ricotta. Roll out the second circle of dough to fit the top on the pie plate. Place it on top of the ricotta and sausage filling, and make sure that the top and bottom crusts are pressed together all around with the tines of a fork. Bake for 1 hour and 15 minutes. Remove from the oven, cover with a cotton towel, and let rest for 30 minutes before cutting and serving.

Variation
SAUSAGE AND RICOTTA ROLL

Scaccia cu' ricotta e sausizza

Serves 6 to 8

My aunt Giovannina Cannizzaro Sirugo rolled the dough into a long rectangle, dotting half of the rectangle on the long side with ricotta, sausage, and bits of lard. She then folded the dough over the filling, pressing the top and the bottom of the crust together all around, placed it in a large lightly greased baking pan, and shaped it like a horseshoe. She would prick the surface with a fork, and bake it in a preheated 375-degree oven for 1 hour and 15 minutes.

SIMPLE FLAKY PASTRY
Sfuogghiu facili

*Serves 6 to 8 or more if cut into smaller portions
for a party or as an appetizer*

*I don't melt the lard as my mother did, instead, I spread it on the
surface of the dough, and then I fold it in thirds as you would fold
a letter. Rest in the refrigerator for 30 minutes.*

Roll it out again into a rectangle with the long side facing you. Dot the surface of the dough with ricotta and sausage meat leaving a 1-inch border all around. Fold about 3 inches of the side nearest you on top of the ricotta and sausage, then carefully fold and roll away from you until you have reached the end of the pastry. You should end up with a thin and long rectangle. Carefully place the roll on a lightly greased baking pan, placing the seam on the bottom. Press both ends together well, then fold them under to be sure that the filling doesn't come out during baking. Brush with beaten egg, and prick the top with a fork. Bake in a preheated 375-degree oven for 1 hour and 15 minutes. Remove from the oven, cover with a cotton towel, and let rest for 30 minutes before cutting and serving.

SWEETS
Cosi aruci

Sweets are the triumphs of the Sicilian kitchen. Convents held the secrets of many traditional desserts that were made by nuns and sold to the public. Sicilian ice cream is still featured all over Italy and is considered the best. Refreshing granita, which is easily made from coffee, fruit juice, or pureed fruits and sugar is known and appreciated all over the world.

Impressive as many of these desserts are, they are relatively simple to prepare, but the presentation of a *cassata*, in all its glory, decorated with candied fruits, still evokes the admiration of one's guests. Yet, *pan di Spagna*, which is the cake in *cassata*, is one of the easiest and most versatile sponge cakes that can be made at home. The basic recipe for this delicious cake can be made into a sheet cake to serve 30 guests, into biscotti, cup-

Caltagirone – Scalinata – The famous staircase of the city.

cakes, and even into a super deluxe ice cream cake. This particular cake can be drenched in liquid such as sweet wine, flavored sugar syrup, brandy, or fruit juice, and it will still hold its shape. It allows you to be as imaginative as you care to be in creating delicious and magnificent desserts.

I can't remember a time when I didn't enjoy cooking. I remember making *zabaglione*, the silkiest and tastiest egg custard imaginable when, as a college student who took studying, cooking, and entertaining seriously, my friends came to visit.

Fried desserts are also wonderful, and they come in a variety of shapes and forms. Most Americans are familiar with the *zeppole*, made from yeast dough, and served during Italian feasts. Although my mother's version is a little different, when I make them, everybody loves them. Doughs made with baking powder yield a different texture, but are just as delicious. Carnival Bows, which are delicious fried ribbons of dough, are another specialty that is hard to resist.

Almonds will appear in many desserts, such as pine nut cookies, *cucciddati*, *granita*, and *marzipan*, which is one of the crowning glories of our ancient but still current cuisine.

PRESERVED ORANGES
Aranci 'ncilippati

Makes 2 pints.

4 seedless oranges, unpeeled

2 cups sugar

¼ cup brandy (optional)

Place the unpeeled oranges in a pot, and cover with cold water, bring to the boil and cook for 2 minutes. Pour off the hot water, fill with cold water, and repeat the process 2 more times to take away the bitterness of the oranges. Take the oranges out of the water, cool, and cut into thick slices reserving the first and the last slice of each orange to make candied orange peel by slicing thinly and cooking in the leftover syrup after the orange slices are done.

Make the syrup by bringing 4 cups water and the sugar to the boil; add the orange slices and cook over low heat for 25 to 35 minutes or until translucent. Place the slices into 2 sterilized wide-mouth pint jars, add syrup to cover and, if you wish, add 2 tablespoons brandy to each jar. Serve on toasted Italian bread for breakfast, or with a scoop of ice cream for dessert.

WHITE PUDDING
Biancu manciari

Serves 8

This was our favorite dessert. My brother Carmelo and I would watch my mother make it, and then we would each get half of the lemon peel that had been cooked in the **biancu manciari** *as a treat.*

Long before **tiramisu** *became the rage, my mother would layer slices of* **pani ri Spagna** *dipped in sweetened coffee with* **biancu manciari,** *for special occasions.*

4 cups milk

¾ cup cornstarch

¾ cup sugar

Peel of 1 lemon, taken off in a long spiral strip

Place 1½ cups milk in a jar with a tight-fitting screw top, add the cornstarch, and shake vigorously to blend the mixture without lumps. Place the remaining 2½ cups milk, the sugar, and lemon peel in a saucepan and heat for 5 minutes. Add the cornstarch mixture while stirring with a wooden spoon. Bring it to the boil, stirring constantly, turn off the heat, remove the lemon peel, and spoon into individual serving bowls or pour into a mold. Chill before serving.

CRULLERS

8 tablespoons butter or
vegetable shortening

1 cup flour

4 eggs

3 cups canola oil

Bring 1 cup water and the butter or shortening to the boil. Add the flour all at once, and stir until the dough comes off the sides of the pan. Remove from the heat, cool for 10 minutes, and add the eggs one at a time, beating the paste until each of the eggs has been absorbed and the paste is smooth.

Heat the canola oil in a medium pan, or in a deep-fryer. Scoop rounded tablespoons of paste, and using your finger or another spoon, to carefully drop the paste into the hot oil. Brown lightly on all sides before placing them on paper towels to drain. Top each *sfinge* with a tablespoon of Sweetened Ricotta (page 143), Ricotta and Candied Fruit Topping (page 144), Ricotta and Chocolate Filling (page 144) or with Pastry Cream (page 143).

CREAM PUFFS

1 recipe Crullers (above)

Preheat the oven to 400 degrees. Either pipe the paste using a plain or a star tip or drop it by rounded tablespoons onto a greased baking pan, and bake for 10 minutes then lower the heat to 350 degrees and bake for another 20 minutes. Cool the cream puff shells, cut in half, and fill with a tablespoon of Sweetened Ricotta (page 143), Ricotta and Candied Fruit Topping (page 144), Ricotta and Chocolate Filling (page 144), Pastry Cream (page 143) or whipped cream.

PASTRY CREAM

Crema pasticciera

Makes 2½ cups

*Use to fill cakes, cream puffs, or to top sfingi (page 142)
instead of ricotta.*

¼ cup cornstarch

2 cups milk

2 egg yolks

¾ cup sugar

Grated peel of 1 lemon (optional)

Dissolve the cornstarch in ½ cup of the milk. Place the remaining 1½ cups milk in a saucepan, add the egg yolks, sugar, and cornstarch mixture. Place over medium heat and stir until thickened. Add the grated lemon peel if using, stir, spoon into a bowl, cool, then chill.

SWEETENED RICOTTA

Ricotta aruci

Makes 1¾ cups

1½ cups ricotta

¼ cup sugar

Beat the ricotta and the sugar with an electric beater until smooth. Use to fill cakes, cream puffs, and crullers.

RICOTTA AND CANDIED FRUIT TOPPING

Ricotta ca' frutta candita

Makes 1¾ cups

1½ cups fresh ricotta

¼ cup sugar

¼ cup chopped candied orange peel, cherries, or candied citron

Beat the ricotta and the sugar with an electric mixer until smooth, add the candied fruit, and refrigerate until ready to use for cakes, cream puffs, or crullers.

RICOTTA AND CHOCOLATE FILLING

Ricotta co' cioccolattu

Makes 1¾ cups

1½ cups fresh ricotta

¼ cup sugar

¼ cup chopped sweet or bittersweet chocolate or small chocolate chips

Beat the ricotta and the sugar with an electric mixer until smooth. Mix in the chocolate with a rubber spatula, and refrigerate until ready to use in cakes, cream puffs, crullers, and cannoli.

CONCETTA'S FRITTERS

Zeppole ri Cuncetta

Serves 8 to 12

2½ cups flour

1 tablespoon instant yeast (see page 7)

1 teaspoon fennel seeds

3 cups canola oil

1 cup sugar

1 teaspoon ground cinnamon

Mix the flour, 1½ cups warm water, yeast, and fennel seeds into a batter. Cover and let rise until tripled in volume, about 1 hour Heat the oil in a deep frying pan, and drop the batter by tablespoonfuls into the hot oil. Turn *zeppole* to brown evenly. Drain on paper towels. Coat the *zeppole* with a mixture of sugar and cinnamon, and serve warm or at room temperature.

RICE AND RAISIN FRITTERS

Friitedde ri risu e passuli

Makes 20 to 24

1½ cups unbleached flour

1 teaspoon instant yeast (see page 7)

1 cup cooked rice

½ cup white raisins

½ cup canola oil

½ cup sugar

Mix the flour, yeast, and 1 cup warm water, and let rise for 1 hour. Mix in the rice and raisins and let rise another hour.

Heat the oil in a large frying pan, and drop the batter by tablespoonfuls, flattening each fritter with the back of a spoon. Fry until delicately browned on one side before turning to brown the other side. Drain on paper towels, and coat with sugar.

FRIED PASTRY SHELLS

Cannuoli

Makes 12

You will need cannoli tubes for this recipe. Look for them at N.Y.Cake & Baking Distributor (1-800-94-CAKE-9) and ask for #CAN923–Small Cannoli Forms or #CAN922–Regular Cannoli Forms. Of course, you can purchase ready-to-fill cannoli shells in Italian markets.

1½ cups flour

2 tablespoons lard or butter

2 tablespoons sugar

1 egg

¼ cup white wine

3 cups canola or other vegetable oil

Ricotta and Chocolate Filling (page 144)

½ cup chopped unsalted pistachios

Cut the lard or butter into the flour, either by hand or by pulsing in a food processor. Add the sugar, egg, and white wine to make a smooth dough. Shape into a ball, coat with a few drops of oil, cover, and let rest for 30 minutes.

Roll the dough into a log, and divide the log into 12 pieces. Shape each piece into a ball. Take each ball and roll into a 4-inch circle. Wrap each circle on a metal cannoli tube overlapping the edges, and lightly pressing them so that they stick together. Deep-fry the pastry on the tubes until delicately browned. Place them on paper towels, and when cool enough to handle, remove the metal tubes. When ready to serve, fill with ricotta filling, and sprinkle the ends with the pistachios.

CARNIVAL BOWS

Scocchi ri carnivali

Serves 8 to 12

3 cups flour

2 eggs

4 tablespoons vegetable oil

½ cup sugar

½ cup white wine

Grated peel of 1 lemon

3 cups canola oil or
   other vegetable oil

¼ cup confectioners' sugar

Mix all the ingredients, except the confectioners' sugar, by hand or using the food processor. Shape into a ball, coat with a few drops of oil, cover with a bowl, and let rest for 30 minutes.

Roll out thinly either by hand or with a pasta machine, rolling it to the next to the last number of thinness. If you are rolling it out with a pasta machine, cut the strips into 1-inch pieces, otherwise cut the sheet of dough into 4 by 1-inch rectangles. Cut a slit in the middle of each one along the long end, and pull one corner through the slit. Fry in the hot canola oil until lightly golden on both sides. Each one will take a different shape. Drain on paper towels, and when ready to serve, dust with confectioners' sugar.

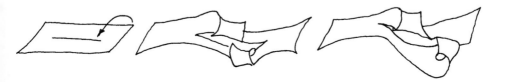

LITTLE FRIED BALLS IN HONEY

'Mpagniuccata

Serves 6 to 8

3 cups flour

4 eggs

Pinch of salt

3 cups canola or
  other vegetable oil

1 cup honey

¼ cup sugar

¼ cup orange water or orange
  juice

Colored sprinkles

Mix the flour, eggs, and salt by hand or in a food processor. Shape into a ball, coat lightly with a few drops of olive oil, cover, and let rest for 30 minutes.

Cut into 4 pieces, and roll each piece into a thin log about 12 inches long. Cut each log into ½-inch pieces, and deep-fry the pieces in hot oil until golden. As you fry them, place on paper towels to absorb the oil.

Heat the honey, sugar, and orange water or orange juice in a large pot that will hold all the fried balls. Add the fried balls, and gently mix to coat each one with honey. Pile the honey-covered balls in a serving platter in a cone shape, and decorate with colored sprinkles.

SADIE'S RICOTTA BALLS

Pasta ri ricotta fritta

Make about 48 fritters using all the batter.

This recipe came from my dear cousin Sadie Battaglia Occhipinti, who was a super cook. Although Sadie was born in the United States, she kept alive the cooking traditions of her mother Neli Biazzo Battaglia, who was my grandmother's sister. Neli immigrated to the United States from Ragusa in 1912, and returned for the first and only time in 1962 to see her sister Concettina after 50 years. Sadie and my grandmother were both born on May 13, and now that they are both gone, I remember them with affection on their special day.

I use Sadie's basic recipe to make fruit-filled fritters. Fry one third of the batter just plain, drop chunks of banana into another third, and drop apple slices into the last third. Each of the fritters will have a characteristic shape: the plain ones are round, the banana fritters are oval, and the apple fritters are long.

3 cups self- rising flour

1 cup plus 2 tablespoons sugar

2 eggs

1 cup milk

½ cup fresh ricotta

1 teaspoon vanilla extract

3 cups of canola or other vegetable oil

Mix the flour, 2 tablespoons sugar, eggs, milk ricotta and vanilla. Drop into hot deep oil by tablespoonfuls. Brown evenly on all sides. Drain on paper towels before rolling in the remaining 1 cup sugar.

Variations on page 150.

Variation
BANANA FRITTERS

Makes 16

Peel 2 bananas and cut each into 8 pieces. Drop the pieces into $\frac{1}{3}$ of the batter to coat, then pick them up with a spoon, and helping yourself with another spoon, drop each banana fritter into the hot oil. Drain on paper towels and roll in sugar.

Variation
APPLE FRITTERS

Makes 16

Slice 2 apples with the skin on, each into 8 slices, dip each piece into $\frac{1}{3}$ of the batter, and proceed as with the banana fritters. Add $\frac{1}{4}$ teaspoon ground cinnamon to the remaining cup of sugar, and coat the apple fritters before serving.

SWEETENED WHEAT BERRIES

Cuccia ri Santa Lucia

Serves 4 to 6

Wheat berries must soak overnight, so plan ahead. They are available at Italian groceries, and from the Baker's Catalogue. See the Appendix.

1 cup wheat berries

2 cups milk

½ cup sugar

Grated peel of 1 lemon

¼ cup honey

¼ cup chopped candied fruit

Place the wheat berries in a pot and cover with cold water plus 2 inches. Bring the water to the boil, cook for 10 minutes, turn off the heat, and let stand overnight.

Place the milk in a pot, add the sugar and grated lemon peel. Bring to the boil, add the drained wheat berries, and simmer very gently, stirring often, until all the milk is absorbed, about 30 minutes. Cool. Spoon onto a serving platter and add the honey, stir, and top with the candied fruits.

ALMOND PASTE FOR COOKIES

Pasta ri mannuli pe' viscotta

Makes enough for 2½ dozen cookies

1 pound almond paste

2 egg whites

1½ cups confectioners' sugar

Mix and knead by hand until you have a smooth paste. Proceed with Pine Nut (page 152) or Almond Orange (page 153) cookies.

PINE NUT COOKIES

Viscotti che' pignoli

Makes 12 cookies

*Use half of the egg white for this recipe,
and the rest for the following one.*

½ recipe Almond Paste for
  Cookies (page 151)

1 egg white, very lightly beaten

¾ cup pignoli (pine nuts)

Preheat oven to 350 degrees. Pinch off pieces of prepared almond paste, roll into balls, coat with egg white, and drop into a small bowl of pignoli so that the pignoli adhere to the top of each cookie. Place the pignoli-coated cookies on a baking tray that has been sprayed, covered with wax or parchment paper, and the paper also sprayed. Bake for 20 minutes. They should <u>barely</u> begin to color; be careful not to burn the pignoli.

ALMOND ORANGE COOKIES

Viscotti ri pasta ri mannuli

Makes 16 cookies

½ recipe Almond Paste for
  Cookies (page 151)

Grated peel of 1 orange

1 egg white

½ cup confectioners' sugar

Mix the orange peel into the almond paste, and roll into 2 logs. Cut each log into 8 pieces, and roll each piece into a ball. When all are done, coat each ball with egg white, and when all have been coated, roll each one in confectioners' sugar. Place the sugar-coated balls on a baking tray that has been sprayed, covered with wax or parchment paper, and sprayed again. Let dry for at least 30 minutes. Preheat the oven to 350 degrees. Pinch the sides of each cookie in 2 directions so as to crack the sugar coating. Bake for 15 minutes.

Variation
CHOCOLATE ALMOND COOKIES

Coat the balls in cocoa powder instead of confectioners' sugar, and make them in the same way.

NINA'S ANISE COOKIES

Viscotti all'anice

Makes 4 dozen cookies

This is my cousin Nina Biazzo Cohen's recipe. Nina draws her cooking expertise from her father's Sicilian and her mother's Russian heritage. Nina's father, my uncle John Biazzo, came to the United States from Ragusa in 1913. He was one of a group of men from Siciliy and from other regions of Italy who married young, progressive, Jewish women. Since Uncle John married an American-born woman, and neither aunt Mary Krenik Biazzo nor my cousins Nina and Joel spoke or understood Italian or Sicilian, I considered them my American relatives. As a child, I thought that the typical American breakfast consisted of bagels, lox, and farmer cheese, and that Thanksgiving turkey was stuffed with kasha (buckwheat groats). Since my father Felice Bellia stuffed turkey with a rice stuffing, it wasn't until I met my Irish mother-in-law, May Murray La Marca, that I had turkey with American bread stuffing.

Anise oil is available in the Baker's Catalogue. See the Appendix.

3½ cups flour

3 teaspoons baking powder

1 cup sugar

⅓ cup olive oil

1 teaspoon anise oil or
  1 tablespoon anise extract

4 eggs, beaten

Mix the flour, baking powder and sugar in a bowl, add the olive oil, anise flavor and eggs, and mix into a soft dough. Turn on to a floured surface, and divide in 4 parts. Roll each part into a 12-inch rope, and cut into 12 pieces. Roll each piece between your hands, and shape into a crescent. Place on sprayed cookie sheets, about 1 inch apart.

Preheat oven to 350 degrees, and bake for 15 to 20 minutes.

Variation

Makes 56 biscotti

Shape the dough into two 14-inch logs, bake 15 to 20 minutes, cut into ½-inch slices, place the slices cut side down in a baking pan, and put back in the oven to toast for 10 minutes.

FRUIT-FILLED COOKIES
Cucciddati

Makes 16 cucciddati

You can purchase Italian sprinkles, also called tens and thousands, at Italian grocery stores.

Pastry

3¾ cups flour

½ cup sugar

½ cup shortening

4 tablespoons butter

1 egg

1 egg yolk

½ cup white wine

Filling

1 ring dried figs (12 to 14 ounces)

½ cup raisins

½ cup candied fruits, chopped

½ cup toasted, chopped almonds

½ cup toasted, chopped filberts

1 tablespoon grated orange peel

1 teaspoon ground cinnamon

1 teaspoon ground cloves

4 ounces sweet or semisweet chocolate, chopped

1 cup honey

Lemon Icing

2 tablespoons lemon juice

1 cup confectioners' sugar

Italian colored sprinkles

For the pastry: Mix all the pastry ingredients by hand or in a food processor. Knead lightly, and let stand covered while you make the filling.

For the filling: Cut away the tough little stems from the figs, and quarter each one. Grind or process the figs, add the raisins, candied fruits, almonds, filberts, orange peel, cinnamon, and cloves, and pulse 4 times. Transfer the mixture to a bowl, add the chocolate and the honey, and mix with a wooden spoon or with your hands until everything is amalgamated. Place the mixture on the counter, divide it into 16 parts. Make a 10 to 12 inch roll out of each portion, and set aside.

For the assembly: Preheat the oven to 375 degrees. Divide the dough into 16 parts. Roll each into a rectangle that will hold one of the

fruit rolls. Place the fruit roll in the center of the dough, and enclose it completely. Roll it with your hands a few times to make it even.

Join the two ends to make a ring. Using a scissors, make cuts along the top of the ring, exposing the filling. Place the *cucciddati* on a greased pan, and bake for 20 minutes.

For the icing: Beat the lemon juice and the sugar to make a spreadable icing. Ice the top of each cooled *cucciddato* and immediately top with colored sprinkles.

RICOTTA TART

1½ pounds ricotta (3 cups)

¾ cup sugar

2 eggs

1 teaspoon ground cinnamon

Pastry from Fruit-Filled Cookies
(page 155) or 2 (9-inch) frozen
deep-dish pie crusts, thawed

Mix the ricotta, sugar, eggs, and cinnamon and refrigerate while you prepare the crust. Preheat the oven to 350 degrees.

If using pastry, divide the dough into 2 portions. Roll out the first piece into a circle that will fit a 9-inch pie plate. Spoon the filling into the pastry-lined pie plate. Roll the second piece of dough into a rectangle, and cut into ½-inch strips. Place 5 of the strips on top of the pie, and another 5 at a diagonal to the first set, to make a lattice. If you are using frozen pie crusts, use 1 crust for the bottom and the other to cut into strips. Bake for 45 to 50 minutes. Cool on a rack.

WHEAT AND RICOTTA PIE

Pastiera ri furmientu e ricotta

Serves 6 to 8

Fiori di Sicilia *is a wonderfully fragrant extract that brings the scents of the island into the American kitchen. It is available from The Baker's Catalogue. See the Appendix.*

Pastry from Fruit-Filled Cookies (page 155) or 1 (9-inch) frozen deep-dish pie crust, thawed

1 (550-gram) jar *grano cotto per pastiera* (cooked wheat for pies) or ½ recipe sweetened Wheat Berries (page 151)

6 eggs

2 cups sugar

2 pounds fresh ricotta cheese

½ cup chopped citron

½ teaspoon *fiori di Sicilia* or 1 teaspoon vanilla extract

If using the pastry, roll into a circle, and line a 9 or 10-inch pie plate with it.

Preheat the oven to 350 degrees. Mix the *grano* with the eggs until the grains are separated. Add the sugar, ricotta citron, and Fiori di Sicilia. Mix well and place the pie shells in a pan to catch any possible drips. Place it on the shelf of the oven, and fill each pie shell to the brim. I do this in the oven so that the filled pies don't have to be moved. Bake for 1¼ hours. Cool on a rack and refrigerate until ready to serve.

SPONGE CAKE

Pani ri Spagna

Makes three 8 to 9-inch cake layers

To eliminate the messy job of buttering pans, use Professional Baking Spray, available from The Baker's Catalogue. I use it in baking, but I also spray cooking utensils for quick and easy clean up. See the Appendix for more information.

6 eggs

1 cup sugar

1 teaspoon vanilla extract

1 cup self-rising flour

Preheat the oven to 350 degrees. Separate the eggs, and place the yolks in one bowl, and the whites in another. Add ½ cup sugar to the yolks. Beat the egg whites with the remaining ½ cup sugar until thick; set aside, and without washing the beaters, start beating the yolks, sugar, and vanilla until thick and lemon colored. Fold the flour into the yolk mixture together with about ⅓ of the egg whites so that the batter doesn't get too thick. Fold in the rest of the whites.

Spoon the batter into three buttered or oil-sprayed round 8 to 9-inch layer cake pans. Bake for 15 to 20 minutes. They are done when they are light gold in color and they shrink away from the sides of the pans. Remove from the oven, cool for 5 minutes, remove the cakes from the pans and cool on a rack.

Variation
PLAIN CUPCAKES

Makes 12

Bake the batter in paper-lined cupcake molds. Fill each one until ⅔ full, and bake in a preheated 350 degree oven for 30 minutes. Cool and dust with powdered sugar.

SICILIAN CAKE

Cassata Siciliana

Serves 12 to 14

Filling

2 cups fresh ricotta

½ cup sugar

½ cup candied fruits, chopped

4 ounces chopped milk or semisweet chocolate or small
chocolate morsels.

1 teaspoon ground cinnamon

Ricotta Icing

2 tablespoons fresh ricotta

2 cups confectioners' sugar

Assembly

1 recipe Sponge Cake (page 158)

1½ cups marsala wine

½ of a whole candied citron

¼ cup candied cherries

½ cup sliced blanched almonds

For the filling: Beat the ricotta and the sugar with an electric mixer until smooth. Divide in half, and add the fruit to one portion and the chocolate and cinnamon to the other. Set aside.

For the icing: Beat the ricotta and the sugar until smooth and of spreading consistency. Set aside.

For the assembly: Place 4 triangles of wax paper on a serving platter under and all around where the cake will be so that the papers can be pulled out after the cake is assembled. Place one cake layer on the wax paper. Place the marsala wine in a small spray bottle, and spray ⅓ on the first layer. Spread the ricotta and fruit filling on top of the cake layer. Place the second layer on top of the ricotta filling, and spray with another ⅓ of the marsala wine. Spread the ricotta and chocolate filling on the second layer, top with the third layer, spray it with the rest of the marsala wine, and let rest.

Place the citron on a cutting board, and slice thinly. Slice the candied cherries in half.

Spread the icing on the top and on the sides of the cake. Press the sliced almonds lightly all over the side of the cake. Place the citron slices in a pattern around the top of the cake, add the cherries, cut side down, to complement the design made by the citron slices. Chill until ready to serve. This is a rich cake, and a small portion is very satisfying.

Variations on pages 160 to 161.

Variation
DECORATIONS

If you are good with a piping bag, you can cover the top and sides of the cake with whipped cream rosettes and decorate it with a few fresh flowers, just before serving, for a spectacular presentation. I grow regular geraniums for the flowers and scented geraniums for the leaves to decorate cakes; in the winter I bring the geraniums indoors to have them on hand. Roses can also be used. Just make sure that no one eats the geraniums or roses because although they are edible, they are not particularly good to eat. Candied violets also make a lovely decoration, and are edible. If you want to really impress your guests, make (page 166) or buy marzipan fruits to decorate your cake.

Variation
ZABAGLIONE CAKE

Substitute Egg and Wine Custard with Cream (page 163) for the Ricotta Cassata filling.

Variation
SHEET CAKE FOR A CROWD

Double the cake recipe and distribute the batter among 3 sheet cake pans (11 by 15 inches). Fill with Ricotta Filling, Egg and Wine Custard with Cream (page 163), or your favorite jam. Frost the cake with Ricotta Icing or whipped cream, decorate it, and serve.

Divided in 3 lengthwise, and then into 1-inch pieces, it will serve 45.

Variation
FILLED PASTRIES

Makes 12 to 16

Make cupcakes (page 158). Cut a cone shape out of the tops of the cupcakes with a small serrated knife. Fill the cavity with Pastry Cream (page 143), Sweetened Ricotta (page 143) or with any of the Ricotta Fillings and Toppings (page 144). Cut the cone-shaped piece you have removed from the cupcake in half. Insert the 2 pieces halfway into the filling so that they stick out and look like butterflies. Dust with powdered sugar.

Variation
BISCOTTI

Makes 50 to 60

My father Felice, the ever inventive cook, would add 1 cup of chopped candied fruits, pignoli, or sliced almonds to the batter, and bake it in a jelly-roll pan. After baking he would cut the cake in half lengthwise, then cut each half into $1/2$-inch slices. He put the slices in the oven, cut side down to toast until barely browned. These are great for those who like to dunk in their coffee.

ICE CREAM CAKE

Cassata gelato

Serves 8 to 12

1 recipe Sponge Cake (page 158), batter only

1 quart ice cream, any flavor, softened

Preheat the oven to 350 degrees. Spoon the batter into a buttered or oil sprayed jelly-roll pan. Bake for 20 minutes. When light golden remove from oven, cool 5 minutes, and remove from pan. Cut cake into 3 equal portions.

Spread softened ice cream between the layers and stack them for a rectangular cake. Frost with Ricotta Icing (page 159) or whipped cream. Freeze until ready to use.

EGG AND WINE CUSTARD

Zabaglione can be served warm, as Italians like it, or chilled, as Americans generally prefer. Zabaglione lightened with whipped cream makes a fabulous cake filling. **Cassata Siciliana** *(page 159) could also be filled with zabaglione.*

4 egg yolks

½ cup sugar

½ cup marsala wine

Place the egg yolks and the sugar in a metal or glass bowl that will fit over a pan of simmering water. Beat the egg yolks until thick. Add the marsala wine, and whisk over the simmering water until the custard falls in a ribbon when the whisk is lifted. Remove from the simmering water, and place in a bowl with ice. Continue to whisk until cold, and refrigerate until ready to serve.

Variation
EGG AND WINE CUSTARD WITH CREAM

Zabaglione ca' panna

Serves 6 to 8

Fold 1 cup whipped heavy cream into the cold custard. This is a very rich dessert. Makes 6 generous servings or 8 smaller portions.

FLAVORED ICES

SUGAR SYRUP

1 cup sugar

Mix sugar with 2 cups water. Bring to the boil, and cook over low heat for 5 minutes. Cool and chill in the refrigerator. Will keep for 1 week.

BASIC GRANITA

Mix the sugar syrup and one of the flavorings indicated below. Place the mixture in a metal ice cube tray and freeze overnight. Break up the frozen mixture, place it in your food processor, and pulse until smooth. Pack in a covered container, and freeze until ready to serve

COFFEE GRANITA

Mix 1 cup of sugar syrup (above) and $3/4$ cup espresso or strong American coffee. Whip $1/2$ cup heavy cream. When ready to serve, top each portion with a dollop of whipped cream.

LEMON, GRAPEFRUIT OR LIME GRANITA

Mix 1 cup sugar syrup (above) and $3/4$ cup lemon, grapefruit or lime juice.

ALMOND-FLAVORED GRANITA

Orzata is an almond syrup available in Italian markets.
The syrup is added to water or to seltzer for a refreshing summer drink.
It also makes delicious granita.

Mix 1 cup sugar syrup (page 164) and ¾ cup orzata.

GRANITA WITH FRUIT PULP

1 cup fruit puree

1 cup sugar syrup (page 164)

Process skinned, ripe fruit such as peaches, apricots, plums, kiwi, or mangoes to make 1 cup. Mix with sugar syrup and freeze as with the other recipes.

MARZIPAN FRUITS

Pasta riale

Makes 18 to 24 depending on size

It has become a much-anticipated annual ritual to attend the marzipan workshop at our Central Unitarian Church in Paramus, New Jersey, on the first Saturday of December. The teacher, Miriam Campo Forbes, is an accomplished marzipan artist and a master bobbin lace maker. She was exposed to these art forms when, as a child, she spent seven months visiting her father's family in Marsala, Sicily. The whole family went to Sicily together, but her father, the Reverend Pietro Campo, had to return to his church in New York City before the rest of the family. He was the minister of the Italian Methodist Episcopal Church, on 114th Street just East of First Avenue, from 1930 to 1944 where he preached in Italian as he ministered to a congregation of Italian and Sicilian immigrants. At the same time and in the same neighborhood, Dr. Leonard Covello, a distinguished writer and educator, was principal of Benjamin Franklin High School. He was the first Italian to be appointed principal of a New York City public school. My husband and I had the pleasure of knowing Dr. Covello, and continued to exchange Christmas cards with him even after he retired to Messina, Sicily.

8 ounces almond paste

1 egg white

2 cups confectioners' sugar, or more

Red, yellow, green and brown food colors

Mix the almond paste and the egg white until smooth. Add 1 cup of powdered sugar and continue to mix making sure there are no lumps. Mix additional sugar until the paste is no longer sticky, but not too dry. Knead it by hand until the paste is very smooth.

To color the almond paste: Take ¼ of the paste and color it light red. Divide it in half, make strawberries with one portion, and add a few drops of yellow to the other portion to make peaches or apricots. Take another ¼ of the paste, and color yellow for pears and bananas. Another ¼ is colored orange for tangerines. The remaining ¼ is colored green, and will be used to make leaves, and green apples.

STRAWBERRIES

Light red-colored almond paste

Red food color

¼ cup red sugar crystals

Green food color

1 ounce whole cloves

Shape light red paste into little cones, paint each of them with red food color, and when all are painted, roll each one in red sugar, and let dry. Paint the tops with green to suggest leaves, and push a whole clove in the middle for the stem.

To color sugar: Place ½ cup sugar in a jar with a tight fitting lid. Add a few drops of liquid food color, mix with a spoon, then cover the jar and shake to distribute the color evenly. This will keep indefinitely.

PEACHES OR APRICOTS

Makes 8 to 12

Peach-colored almond paste

Diluted red food color

Toothpick for details

Shape the peaches or apricots by making balls with a point, make an indentation on the top opposite the point, then crease with the sides of a toothpick to make it look like a peach or an apricot. Make the blush on the peach or apricot by painting with a small brush or by using your finger, placing a touch of diluted red color on the peach or apricot, and blending it from light to dark.

PEARS

Makes 8 to 12

Yellow-colored almond paste

Whole cloves

Diluted red food color

Shape the pears, stick a whole clove as a stem, and another at the other end so that you see only the bud of the clove. Paint a red blush, as for the peaches, using diluted red food color, or dab on with your finger, blending the color from light to dark.

BANANAS

Yellow-colored almond paste

Diluted brown food color

Very fine brush

Roll small pieces of paste and flatten each roll on the three sides. Curve slightly, and flatten one end. Use a small brush to paint brown lines and spots to look like ripe bananas.

ORANGES OR TANGERINES

Makes 8 to 12

Orange-colored almond paste

Fine box or hand grater

Orange food color

Small brush and toothpick

Shape several pieces of the paste into balls and roll each one on a fine grater to texture the surface. Paint each one with orange food color, let dry, then make a little indentation on the top with a toothpick, and make little creases around the little hole.

LEAVES AND APPLES

Makes 18 to 14 leaves and 8 to 12 apples

Green-colored almond paste

Small leaf cutters

Small knife

Tiny rolling pin or an inch piece of a ³⁄₄-inch dowel to flatten the almond paste

Roll out ½ of the green paste, cut out leaf shapes either by hand or with a canapé or cookie cutter, and set aside to decorate the platter when ready to serve the marzipan. Gather up the trimmings, add to the last portion of green paste, and shape the apples.

Keep the marzipan fruits in an airtight container. They will stay soft for one month.

FEAST DAY MENUS
Menu' pe' festi

JANUARY 1

New Year's Day

L'Annu Nuovu

Lentil Soup with Homemade Pasta (page 56)
Lentils with Broccoli (page 119)
Sausage in Wine (page 89)
Crusty Bread (page 35)
Fruit-Filled Cookies (page 155)
Sicilian Cake (page 159)

NEW YEAR'S DAY

My earliest memory of a holiday tradition in Sicily is visiting, with my little brother Carmelo, our grandfather Don Giovannino on New Year's Day, respectfully kissing his hand, and receiving *a strina*, a gift of money. The several coins, at our young age of 4 and 6, seemed like great riches. Our grandfather would then tell us of his childhood memories of visiting his own grandfather, receiving his coins, and being treated to a breakfast of thinly cut pan-fried pork chops with slices of bread browned in the pan drippings. My mother and my uncles remember this family tradition. Lentils that resemble the shape of coins, are the symbol of prosperity, and are always included in the menu for New Year's Day.

170

SICILIAN FEASTS

MARCH 19
Feast of Saint Joseph and Father's Day
San Giuseppi e a Festa re Padri

Sicilian Rice Balls (page 20)
Chickpeas with Fennel (page 118)
Stuffed Mushrooms (page 19)
Oven-Dried Tomatoes (page 14)
Cheese Tray with Pears
Sun-Shaped Bread (page 34)
Concetta's Fritters (page 145)
Saint Joseph's Crullers (page 142)

FEAST OF SAINT JOSEPH AND FATHER'S DAY

March 19 is a very special day. The feast of Saint Joseph is also Father's Day in all of Italy. Traditionally, Sicilian families set great tables and food was offered to the poor and to whom ever came by. Breads in decorative shapes were made, and as many dishes were prepared as could be afforded by the host families. Naturally these grand tables were prepared by the well to do to serve as an offering to their community. If you go to any of the "Little Italies" in the United States, all the bakeries will have *zeppole* and *sfingi di San Giuseppe* that are fried and sugar-coated dough and pastries filled with ricotta or custard. At our house, both in Sicily and in the United States, my mother Concetta prepared our favorite *zeppole* (fritters), which were made with a yeast dough and fennel seeds, deep-fried, and coated with sugar and cinnamon.

EASTER SUNDAY

Pasqua

Easter is the most special holiday of the year. In 1986 during my sabbatical leave from The Bronx High School of Science where I taught art and where I introduced Italian, I had the pleasure of spending Easter in Ragusa when I accompanied my mother Concetta for her annual trip. Early on Easter morning, my cousin Carola Distefano, took me to see a unique Easter Sunday festival and procession in the city of Modica. The feast, called A Maronna Vasa Vasa, (*vasa* means "kiss") commemorates the three meetings, and the exchange of three kisses, by the risen Christ and his mother Mary on Easter Sunday. Fully articulated life-sized figures of Christ and the Madonna are taken in procession, and after their last kiss, they turn and bless the people in the *piazza*, in front of the church of Santa Maria Delle Grazie. We were able to enjoy the whole event from a balcony right on the piazza overlooking the beautiful church.

We returned to Ragusa for a spectacular Easter dinner that had been prepared by Zia Lucia Di Martino Sirugo, with the help of her daughters, my cousins Carmela Sirugo La Terra and Gianfranca Sirugo Corallo. The family around the holiday table, the fragrances of the very special dinner, brought back a rush of memories of the festive gatherings that I remembered from my childhood. Zia Lucia's *'mpanata* eagerly anticipated with joy after the long and lean Lenten period, was as delicious as any I had ever eaten. After a sumptuous dinner, which lasted for hours, my cousin's children, Antonietta La Terra and Mirko Corallo, broke the big chocolate easter egg, as their grandfather, Zio Nini' Sirugo, and my mother, treated us to stories from their childhood. With my mother gone, we still delight in Zio Nini's incomparable storytelling, which we look forward to and enjoy to this day during frequent telephone conversations and visits to Ragusa. The sights, scents, and tastes of this particular Easter, made the day truly memorable.

PASQUETTA

Molded Macaroni *(page 72)*
Sausage and Ricotta Pie *(page 136)*
Grilled Eggplant with Mint Sauce *(page 114)*
Homemade Rolls *(page 34)*
Rice and Raisin Fritters *(page 145)*
Ricotta Tart *(page 156)*
Cream Puffs *(page 142)*

Pasquetta is a national holiday. Everybody takes some of the delectable leftovers of the Easter feast, and dishes that are made especially for this day, and shares them with family and friends in their country house or at the seashore. In March and April, the Sicilian countryside is blanketed with wild flowers of every shape and color. I still delight in my childhood memories of afternoon walks in the country with my mother and little brother. The last time I visited Sicily in the spring, I relived those lovely days and discovered that my mind's eye had not exaggerated the beauty, the variety, and the brilliant colors of the Sicilian wild flowers of my childhood.

AUGUST 15

Ferragosto

Folded Parsley Bread (page 130)
Sausage and Ricotta-Filled Rolls (page 38)
Leek and Ricotta Pie (page 135)
Sliced Fennel
Dried Salted Ricotta Cheese
Caciocavallo Cheese
Prickly Pears (page 9)
Nina's Anise Cookies (page 154)

August 15 is a national holiday that celebrates the feast of the Assumption. In our family it was a special day because it was my father's birthday. In fact, since he was born on this important religious holiday, he was given the name Felice Maria Bellia. My mother was also born on an important religious holiday in the same year as my father, in 1909. She was born on December 8, the feast of the Immaculate Conception, so although she would have been given, as the first born, the name of her paternal grandmother, my great-grandmother, Giorgia, who was a very devout woman, insisted that she be called Concetta. I also got my name by accident of birth. According to custom and tradition, I should have been named Concetta after my paternal grandmother, but having been born prematurely and weighing only 600 grams (1 pound 3 ounces), fearing that I might not survive, I was baptized immediately after birth, and was given the name Giovanna after the patron saint of Ragusa, San Giovanni Battista (Saint John the Baptist).

August 15 is also the beginning of summer vacations for many in Italy and in Sicily. *Ferragosto* is a holiday when no self-respecting Italian would be caught dead at home in the city! Everybody heads out for a country picnic leaving the cities completely to the tourists.

SICILIAN FEASTS

NOVEMBER 2

Marzipan Fruits (page 166)
Fried Pastry Shells (page 146)
Fresh Fruits
Nuts

All Souls' Day is the annual day of remembrance for each family's dearly departed. When children go to bed on the eve of November 2, they look forward to finding little treats when they awake the following morning, gifts from their departed ancestors. Rather than this being a sad day, it's a day when family members and friends who have died are fondly remembered, trips are made to the cemeteries, flowers are brought to the graves and people socialize as they honor their dead.

I remember one day when *I Murticieddi*, which roughly translates as the dear little dead ones, left a marzipan prickly pear for my little brother Carmelo who was afraid to touch it because it looked so real! Prickly pears are a very sweet fruit that, in nature, are covered with thorns. Although the thorns are removed before they are sold, some invariably remain, and as children we were not allowed to touch them. Little Carmelo wasn't sure if it was a trick or a treat.

NOVEMBER 3
Birthday of Vincenzo Bellini
Cumpliannu ri Vincenzu Bellini

Pasta with Eggplant (page 71)
Orange and Fennel Salad (page 123)
Homemade Rolls (page 34)
Lemon Granita (page 164)

November 3 is the anniversary of the birth of the famous composer Vincenzo Bellini. Born in 1801 in the city of Catania, we honor the memory of this beloved Sicilian musician with the delicious dish, *Pasta alla Norma* named for the main character of his Bel Canto opera masterpiece, *Norma*.

DECEMBER 13
Feast of Saint Lucy's Day
Festa ri Santa Lucia

Sweetened Wheat Berries (page 151)
Pine Nut Cookies (page 152)
Almond Orange Cookies (page 153)
Egg and Wine Custard with Cream (page 163)

On December 13, Sicilians commemorate the miracle of Saint Lucy. When the people of Siracusa, who were on the verge of starvation, prayed to Saint Lucy, their patron saint, their prayers were answered when a ship full of wheat berries arrived in the port. To satisfy their hunger as quickly as possible, people didn't take the time to grind the wheat into flour. So, sweet and savory dishes made from whole, cooked wheat berries known as *Cuccia* became traditional on Saint Lucy's Day. This beloved Saint continues to be honored on her feast day, and foods made with <u>wheat</u> flour are not prepared and eaten on December 13.

DECEMBER 24

Christmas Eve

Vigilia ri Natali

Penne with Cauliflower (page 69)
Calamari with Tomato Sauce (page 103)
Tuna with Onions (page 103)
Dried Cod Stew (page 106)
Potato, Pepper, and Onion Casserole (page 117)
Sautéed Broccoli Rape (page 110)
Scallion and Caper Salad (page 126)
Baked Flat Bread (page 30)
Sadie's Ricotta Balls (page 149)

The Christmas Eve menu is made up of a variety of fish dishes. There can be as few as 3 to signify the Trinity, and in some families, as many as 12 to signify the 12 Apostles.

DECEMBER 25

Christmas Day

Natali

Chicken Soup with Tiny Meatballs and Egg Noodles (page 48)
Stuffed Chicken Legs (page 91)
Meats in Aspic (page 97)
Carrots with Capers (page 117)
Romaine and Cucumber Salad (page 124)
Dried Fruits and Nuts
Preserved Oranges (page 141)
White Pudding (page 141)

Christmas in Sicily is a religious family holiday. A festive dinner is enjoyed by family and guests but without any excesses. Gifts are exchanged on January 6, the day of the Epiphany, and they are brought by the *Befana*, a good and friendly witch who flies through the air on her broomstick.

Try these sources for authentic Italian equipment and ingredients.

Agata & Valentina
1505 First Avenue
New York, NY 10021
(212) 452-0690

Arthur Avenue and 187th Street is a hub of shops and restaurants in the most authentic Little Italy in New York City. Near the Bronx Zoo, the New York Botanical Gardens, the Enrico Fermi Cultural Center and Library, and Fordham University, it provides first class shopping, food, culture, and entertainment.

Arthur Avenue Market, one of the few remaining enclosed city markets
2344 Arthur Avenue
Bronx, NY
(718) 367-5688

Borgatti
632 East 187th Street
Bronx, NY
(718) 298-6105
The Bogatti family has been making fresh pasta daily since 1935. Fresh egg, spinach, carrot, tomato and whole wheat pasta available every day except Monday, and always with tips and recipes.

Calandra Cheese Shop
2314 Arthur Avenue
Bronx, NY
(718) 365-7572
Ricotta and mozzarella are made fresh every day. The first time I bought ricotta there, a customer was told never to cover the ricotta in the refrigerator, and when she said that it might pick up off flavors from the other foods, she was told with great passion "then cover the other foods!"

Egidio Pastry Shop
620 East 187th Street
Bronx, NY 10458
(718) 295-6077
There you can enjoy espresso or cappuccino with their own cookies, biscotti or pastries.

Madonia Bakery
2348 Arthur Avenue
Bronx, NY
(718) 295-5573

The Baker's Catalogue
King Arthur Flour
PO Box 876
Norwich, VT 05055-0876
800- 827-6836
www.bakerscatalogue.com

Bergen Marzipan and Chocolate Inc.
205 South Washington Avenue
Bergenfield, New Jersey 07621
(201) 385-8343

Corrado's
1578 Main Avenue
Clifton, NJ 07011
(973) 340-0628
Outstanding selection of Italian fruits, vegetables, meats, cheeses, and fish.
www.corradosmarket.com

D'Artagnan
800-327-8246
www.dartagnan.com
Great source for game, quail, rabbit, and more.

Ferdinando's Focacceria Ristorante
151 Union Street
Brooklyn, NY 11231
(718) 855-1545
*Authentic Sicilian restaurant owned and run by the same
family since 1904.*

Jerry's Gourmet & More (two locations)
410 South Dean Street
Englewood, NJ 07631
(201) 871-7108
656 21st Street
Miracle Mile Plaza
Vero Beach, FL 32960
(772) 794-5454

Manganaro
488 9th Avenue
New York, NY 10018
www.manganaros.com
Ships cheeses, fresh mozzarella and cold cuts.

New York Cake & Baking Distributor
56 West 22nd Street
New York, NY 10010
(212) 675-CAKE
1-800-94-CAKE-9

Williams-Sonoma
P.O. Box 379900
Las Vegas, NV 89137-9900
(800) 541-2233
www.williams-sonoma.com

Zabar's
2245 Broadway (at 80th St.)
New York, NY 10024
800-697-6301
www.zabars.com
A New York institution for the best coffees, cheeses, breads, smoked fish, meats, prepared foods, and a vast selection of cooking equipment

For more information about The Ibla Grand Prize:
Dr. Salvatore Moltisanti
Ibla International Music Foundation
226 East 2nd Street, Suite 5D
New York, NY 10009
www.ibla.org

My generation spoke the Sicilian language from birth, but when we started school, the instruction was in standard Italian from the very first day. All Italians were at one time bilingual. Unfortunately, the dialects are no longer spoken in every home, and a cultural and linguistic treasure has been lost. Although Sicily has substantial literature and a wonderful literary tradition, we were never taught to read and to write it. Those who did learn to read and write the language did so individually because of personal interest.

The Sicilian language is a very intimate means of communication and self-expression. As I was growing up in the United States, I spoke Sicilian to my parents, English to my brother, Italian to friends from Italy and even Sicilians whom I didn't know intimately. After I was married and had a child, I spoke Italian to my daughter Nicoletta, since I wanted her to have the advantage of being bilingual, and English to my husband Howard. Our daughter, who is a talented linguist, learned Sicilian from my mother, during her many stays in Ragusa while she was growing up.

From her grandmother Concetta Sirugo Bellia, and from her great-grandmother Concettina Biazzo Bellia, she got her love for Sicily and her knowledge of the language. This was further reinforced by the fact that she has "a twin cousin" in Ragusa. Antonietta La Terra was born in Ragusa to my first cousin Carmela Sirugo La Terra, on September 29, 1968, and on the same day, Nicoletta was born in Englewood, New Jersey. Incredibly, Nicoletta and Antonietta each had a baby on March 11, 1998. Nicoletta's son Felice was born in Teaneck, New Jersey, and Antonietta's daughter Ludovica was born in Ragusa.

Nicoletta and Felice   *Antonietta and Ludovica*

The pronunciation of Sicilian is like Italian in that the vowels are pure, and are pronounced in the same way no matter where they occur in a word. Sicilian words will sometimes have a double consonant to indicate stress on that syllable.

The sounds of the vowels are:

a as in await
e as in every
i as in igloo
o as in open
u as in duet

In **ce** and **ci**, the **c** sounds like the **ch** as in **ch**urch
In **ca**, **co**, **cu**, **che**, **chi**, the **c** sounds like the **ch** in chorus
In **ge** and **gi**, the **g** sound like the **g** in **g**entle
In **ghe**, **ghi**, **ga**, **go**, **gu**, the **g** sounds like the **g** in **ghe**to

GLOSSARY

SICILIAN ITALIAN ENGLISH

SICILIAN	ITALIAN	ENGLISH
Acciu ca' casola	Sedano con fagioli	Celery with beans
Agghiu e uogghiu	Aglio e olio	Garlic and oil
Agnieddu arrustutu	Agnello arrostito	Roasted lamb
Anciuovi	Anciovi	Anchovies
Arancini	Arancini	Rice balls
Aranci e finuocci a 'nzalata	Arance e finocchi ad insalata	Orange and fennel salad
Aranci 'ncilippati	Arance sciroppate	Preserved oranges
Baccala' a spizzatinu	Baccala' a spezzatino	Stewed salt cod
Biancu manciari	Bianco mangiare	White milk pudding
Bigne'	Bigne'	Cream puffs
Bruocculi che' pinne	Broccoli con penne	Broccoli with penne
Bruocculi rapi	Broccoli rape	Broccoli rape
Bruoru	Brodo	Broth
Bruoru ri iaddina	Brodo di gallina	Chicken broth
Bruoru ri pisci	Brodo di pesce	Fish broth
Bruoru ri pisci co' risu	Brodo di pesce con riso	Fish broth with rice
Caciu frittu	Formaggio fritto	Fried cheese
Calamari co' pummaroru	Calamari col pomodoro	Squid with tomato
Cannuoli	Cannoli Siciliani	Cannoli (fried shells)
Capunatina	Caponata	Eggplant relish
Capunatina che' crustini	Crostini con caponata	Toasts with caponata
Carciuofuli cini	Carciofi ripieni	Stuffed artichokes
Casola cu' l'acciu	Fagioli con sedano	Beans with celery
Cassata Siciliana	Cassata Siciliana	Sicilian cake
Causunedda	Cavatelli	Handmade pasta
Ciciri che' finuocci	Ceci con finocchi	Chickpeas with fennel
Cicuoria frisca	Cicoria fresca	Fresh dandelions
Cimi ri rape affugati	Cime di rape al vapore	Steamed broccoli rape
Cipudda pipi e patati	Cipolla peperoni e patate	Onions, peppers, and potatoes

Cipuddi fritti	Cipolle fritte	Fried onions
Cosci ri iaddina ca' sarsa	Cosce di gallina con salsa	Chicken legs with sauce
Cosci ri iaddina cini	Cosce di gallina farcite	Stuffed chicken legs
Coscia ri agnieddu arrustuta	Coscia di agnello arrosto	Roasted leg of lamb
Crema pasticciera	Crema pasticcera	Pastry cream
Cruscenti	Biga oppure lievito	Yeast sponge
Cuccia	Grano cotto	Cooked wheat berries
Cucciddati	Biscotti ripieni di frutta	Fruit-filled cookies
Cucuzzeddi c'acitu	Zucchini all'aceto	Zucchini with vinegar
Cucuzzeddi fritti	Zucchini fritti	Fried zucchini
Cuddureddi	Panini	Homemade rolls
Cumpanagghiu	Companatico	Accompaniment to bread
Cunigghiu o iaddina a ghiotta	Coniglio o gallina a ghiotta	Stewed rabbit or chicken
Cuostuli	Costole	Spare ribs
Cuscus Trapanese	Cuscus Trapanese	Couscous from Trapani
Cutini ri maiali cini	Cotenne di maiale farcita	Stuffed pork skins
Cutugnata	Cotognata	Quince jam
Farsumagru	Fetta di manzo farcita	Stuffed beef roll
Fedde ri pani fritti	Fette di pane fritte	Fried bread slices
Feddi ri pani fritti co' 'zuccuru	Fette di pane fritte con zucchero	Fried bread slices with sugar
Ficupali	Fichi d'India	Prickly pears
Finuocci e aranci a 'nzalata	Finicchio e arance in insalata	Fennel and orange salad
Frittata	Frittata	Frittata or omelet
ri cipudda e patati	di cipolla e patate	with onions and potatoes
ri patati e cipudda	di patate e cipolla	with potatoes and onions
ri bruocculi rapi	di cime di rape	with broccoli rape
Frittedde ri risu e passuli	Frittelle di riso ed uvetta	Rice and raisins fritters
Funci cini	Funghi ripieni	Stuffed mushrooms
Frutta martorana	Frutti di pasta di mandole	Marzipan fruits
Granita	Granita	Ices
Iaddina ca' lumia	Pollo al limone	Chicken with lemon sauce
Lasagneddi	Fettuccine	Broad egg noodles
Liatina	Gelatina di carne	Meats in aspic

Linticcia	Lenticchia	Lentils
Linticcia che' sciuriddi	Lenticchie con cavolfiore	Lentils with cauliflower
Maccu ri favi	Purea di fave	Fava beans puree
Matalugghia fritta	Pasta fritta o Torta fritta	Fried bread dough
Merenda	Merenda	After-school snack
Minesra ri casola co' risu	Minestra di fagioli con riso	Bean soup with rice
ri cucuzzedda	di zucchini	Zucchini soup
ri sciuriddi e ricotta	di cavolfiore e ricotta	Cauliflower and ricotta soup
ri sparici	di asparagi	Asparagus soup
ri virdura	di verdura	Vegetable soup
Mufuletta	Pane rotondo	Round flattened loaf
Mulinciana 'ncaciata	Melanzana col cacio	Eggplant layered with cheese
Mulinciana ca' menta	Melanzana alla menta	Eggplant with mint
Muorica – citta' 'nta pruvincia ri Rausa	Modica - Citta' in provincia di Ragusa	Modica – city in the province of Ragusa
Murruzzu sapuritu	Merluzzo saporito	Cod with garlic and parsley
'Mpagniuccata	Palline di pasta fritte	Fried dough balls in honey
'Mpanata Rausana	Torta di agnello Ragusana	Lamb pie from Ragusa
'Nzalata ri aranci	Insalata di arance	Orange salad
ri aranci e finuocci	arance e finocchi	Orange and fennel salad
ri cipudduzzi	di cipolline o scalogne	Scallion salad
ri citriolu e putrisinu	di cetriolo e prezzemolo	Cucumber and parsley salad
ri lattuca e citriolu	di lattuga e cetriolo	Lettuce and cucumber salad
ri patati e cipuddi	di patate e cipolle	Potato and onion salad
ri pummaroru	di pomodoro	Tomato salad
Ova fritti ca' sarsa	Uova fritte nella salsa	Eggs fried in sauce
Pallottoline po' bruoru	Polpettine per il brodo	Little meatballs for soup
Panelle	Frittelle di farina di ceci	Chickpea flour fritters
Pani	Pane	Bread
Pani 'ntricciatu	Pane intrecciato	Braided bread
a forma ri suli	a forma di sole	Sun-shaped bread
ca' marmellata	con la marmellata	Bread and jam

co' zuccuru	con lo zucchero	Bread with sugar
cu l'ova	cotto con uova sode	Bread baked with hard-boiled eggs
Pani cu' cioccolattu	Pane con la cioccolata	Bread with chocolate
cu' l'uogghiu	con l'olio – fettunta	Bread with oil
cunzatu	condito	Seasoned bread
cunzatu fatto 'ncasa	condito fatto in casa	Homemade seasoned bread
frittu a fedde	Fette di pane fritte	Fried bread slices
frittu co' zuccuru	Pane fritto con lo zucchero	Fried bread with sugar
rattatu abbrustulitu	grattuggiato abbrustolito	Toasted bread crumbs
ri Spagna	Pan di Spagna	Italian sponge cake
Pasta 'mpastata	Pasta impastata	Homemade egg noodles
alla Norma	alla Norma	Pasta with eggplant
c'anciuovi	con anciovi	Pasta with anchiovies
ca' linticcia	e lenticchie	Lentil soup
che' sardi	con sarde	Pasta with sardines
che' ciciri	con i ceci	Chickpeas Soup
che' patati	con le patate	Potato soup
cu l'agghiu e l'uogghiu	con aglio ed olio	Pasta with garlic and oil
cu l'ova e cucuzzeddi	con uova e zucchini	Zucchini and egg soup
pa' pizza	per la pizza	Pizza dough
pe' scacci	per focacce	Focaccia dough
pe' Tomasini	per Tomasini	Dough for Tomasini
ri Muorica	di Modica	from the city of Modica
reale	di mandorle	Almond paste
ri pani	per il pane	Bread dough
ri ricotta fritta	di ricotta fritta	Fried ricotta dough
sfogghia	sfoglia	Flaky pastry
Pastiera ri furmientu e ricotta	Torta di frumento e ricotta	Wheat and ricotta pie
Pastina minuta minuta	Pastina piccola piccola	Tiny pasta for soup
Patacchi	Topinambour	Jerusalem artichokes
Patati 'nfurnati	Patate infornate	Baked potatoes
Patati pipi e cipudda	Patate peperoni e cipolle	Potatoes, onions, and peppers

Patati pipi e sausizza	Patate peperoni e salsiccia	Potatoes peppers and sausage
Pinni che' bruocculi	Penne con broccoli	Penne with broccoli
Pipi arrustuti	Peperoni arrostiti	Roasted peppers
Piscispada co' salmurigliu	Pescaspada con Salmoriglio	Swordfish with Salmoriglio
Pizza c'anciuovi	Pizza con gli anciovi	Anchovy pizza
Pizza ca' ricotta	Pizza con la ricotta	Pizza with ricotta
Pizza che' cucuzzeddi	Pizza con zucchini	Pizza with zucchini
Prisella ca' menta	Piselli con la menta	Peas with mint
Pumarori salati	Pomodori salati	Salted dried tomatoes
Purpetti	Polpette	Meatballs
Ragu' ri carni	Sugo di carne	Meat sauce
Ragu' ra ruminica	Sugo della domenica	Sunday meat sauce
Ricotta arriminata	Ricotta mescolata	Ricotta sauce
Ripienu pe' Tomasini	Ripieno per i Tomasini	Filling for Tomasini
Salmurigliu	Salsa di olio e limone	Oil and Lemon sauce
Sardi fritti	Sarde fritte	Fried sardines
Sardi 'nfurnati co' caciu	Sarde infornate col formaggio	Baked sardines with cheese
Sarsa che' cosci ri iaddina	Salsa con le coscie di pollo	Sauce with chicken thighs
crura	Salsa cruda	Uncooked tomato sauce
piccanti	Salsa piccante	Spicy tomato sauce
ri agghiu e uogghiu	Salsa di aglio ed olio	Garlic and oil sauce
ri anciuovi	Salsa di anciovi	Anchovy sauce
ri pummarori	Salsa di pomodoro	Tomato sauce
ri putrisinu	Salsa di prezzemolo (Salsa verde)	Parsley sauce (green sauce)
ri tunnu	Salsa di tonno	Tuna sauce
Sausizza	Salsiccia	Sausage
Sausizza ca' sarsa	Salsiccia con salsa	Sausage in tomato sauce
Sausuzza co' vinu	Salsiccia al vino	Sausage cooked in wine
Scaccia ca' spinacia	Focaggia di spinaci	Spinach pie
co' basilico'	Focaccia al basilico	Folded bread with basil
co' putrisinu	Focaccia al prezzemolo	Folded parsley bread
ri bruocculi	Focaccia di broccoli	Broccoli and sausage pie
e sausizza	e salsiccia	

ri puorri e ricotta	Focaccia di porri e ricotta	Leek and ricotta pie
ri spinaci e patacchi	Focaccia di spinaci e topinambour	Spinach and Jerusalem artichokes pie
Scarola agghiu e uogghiu	Scarola con aglio ed olio	Dandelions with garlic and oil
Sciuri ri cucuzzeddi fritti	Fiori di zucca fritti	Fried zucchini flowers
Sciuriddi ca' linticcia	Cavolfiore con le lenticchie	Cauliflower with lentils
Sciuriddi fritti	Cavolfiore fritto	Fried cauliflower
Scocchi ri carnivali	Fiocchi di carnevale— Cenci	Fried bows
Sfinciuni Palermitanu	Pizza Palermitana	Pizza from Palermo
Sfingi ri San Giuseppi	Sfingi di San Giuseppe	Fritters of Saint Joseph
Sfuogghiu ca' ricotta	Pasta sfoglia con la ricotta	Flaky ricotta pie
Spaghetti che cimi ri rapi	Spaghetti con cime di rape	Spaghetti with broccoli rape
Sparici	Asparagi	Asparagus
Spizzatinu ri baccala'	Spezzatino di baccala'	Salted cod stew
Spizzatinu ri patati cu l'ova	Spezzatino di patate ed uova	Potato and egg stew
A strina	La Strenna	Gift of money for New Year
Taghiarini	Tagliatelle	Fine egg noodles
Timballu ri pasta	Timballo di pasta	Molded macaroni
Trippa ca' prisella	Trippa con piselli	Tripe with peas
Tunnu ca' cipudda	Tonno fresco con cipolla	Tuna with onion
Ulivi cunzati	Olive condite	Olive salad
Ulivi fritti	Olive fritte	Fried olives
Vastunachi che' ciapparieddi	Carote con capperi	Carrots with capers
Viscotti che' pignoli	Biscotti ai pignoli	Pine nut cookies
Viscotti ri pasta ri mannuli	Biscotti di pasta di mandorle	Almond paste cookies
Zabaglione	Zabaglione	Wine and egg custard
Zeppole	Zeppole – Frittelle	Fritters

Basile, Gaetano. Sicilian Cuisine through History and Legend. translated by Gaetano Cipolla, in Arba Sicula, 1998.

Bugialli, Giuliano. Foods of Sicily & Sardinia And The Smaller Islands. Rizzoli, New York, 1996.

Buono come il Pane. The Bronx High School of Science, New York, 1982.

Cosentini, Gaetano. Gli "Aurei Consigli" di Archestrato. Iblea Grafica, Editrice, Ragusa

Lanza, Anna Tasca. The Heart of Sicily. Clarkson Potter/Publishers, New York, 1993.

———. The Flavors of Sicily. Clarkson Potter/Publishers, New York, 1996.

Muffoletto, Anna. The Art of Sicilian Cooking. Gramercy Publishing Company, New York, 1982.

di Pirajno, Alberto Denti. Siciliani a Tavola. Longanesi & C., Milano, 1970.

Pupella, Eufemia Azzolina. Sicilian Cookery. Casa Editrice Bonechi, Florence, 1996.

Schiavelli, Vincent. Papa Andrea's Sicilian Table. Carol Publishing Group, Birch Lane Press, New York N.Y., 1993

Simeti, Mary Taylor. Pomp And Sustenance. Alfred A. Knopf, New York, 1989.

———. Bitter Almonds. William Morrow and Company, Inc. New York, 1994.

di Lampedusa Giuseppe Tomasi. Il Gattopardo. Feltrinelli, Milano, Italy, 1958-1962.

———. The Leopard. translated by Archibald Colquhoun, Pantheon Books Inc., New York, NY, 1960.

Tornabene, Wanda and Giovanna. La Cucina Siciliana di Gangivecchio. Alfred A. Knopf, New York, 1996.

——. Sicilian Home Cooking. Alfred A. Knopf, New York, 2001.

Veronelli, Luigi. Sicilia. Aldo Garzanti Editore, s.a.s., Milano,1970.

Continued

O

Oil
  Bread with Oil, 33
  Escarole with Oil and Garlic, 116
  and Garlic Sauce, 79
  and Lemon Sauce, 77
  Spaghetti with Garlic and Oil, 67
Olives
  Fried Black, 15
  Green Olive Salad, 15
Onion(s)
  Fried for Pizza, 40
  Frittata with Onions and Potatoes, 23
  Onion, Potato, and Pepper
    Casserole, 117
  and Potato Salad, 126
  and Tomato Salad, 125
  Tuna with Onions, 103
Orange(s)
  Almond Orange Cookies, 153
  and Fennel Salad, 123
  Preserved, 141
  Salad, 123
Oven-Dried Tomatoes, 14

P

Parsley
  Cod with Garlic and Parsley, 102
  and Cucumber Salad, 125
  Folded Parsley Bread, 130
  Sauce, 78
Pasta, 61-73
  Broad and Fine Egg Noodles, 64
  Chicken Soup with Tiny Meatballs
    and Egg Noodles, 48
  with Eggplant, 71
  with Fennel and Sardines, 70
  Handmade, 65
  Homemade, 63
  Linguine with Anchovies, 68
  Molded Macaroni, 72
  Pasta, Rice, Ricotta and Cauliflower
    Soup, 51
  Penne with Cauliflower, 69

Pasta (continued)
  Processor Pastina, 65
  Ravioli, 73
  Semolina Noodles, 50
  Spaghetti with Broccoli Rape, 66
  Spaghetti with Garlic and Oil, 67
Pastry
  Cream, 143
  Flaky, Simple, 138
  Shells, Fried, 145
Peas
  with Mint, 114
  Molded Macaroni, 72
  Tripe with Peas, 96
Pizza
  with Anchovies, 41
  Dough, 40
  of Palermo, 43
  Sicilian, 41
  White, 42
Poached Eggs Sicilian-Style, 25
Pork Skins, Stuffed, 85
Potato(es)
  and Egg Stew, 25
  Frittata with Onions and Potatoes, 23
  and Onion Salad, 126
  Oven-Browned, 116
  Potato, Pepper, and Onion
    Casserole, 117
  Potatoes, Sausage, and Peppers, 89
  Soup, 52
Processor Pastina, 65
Pudding, White, 141

Q

Quince Jam, 32

R

Raisin and Rice Fritters, 145
Ravioli from Ragusa, 73
Rice
  Asparagus Soup with Rice, 49
  Balls, 20
  Fish Soup with Rice, 59